'Mark has, in his captivating style, captured the need to apply the power of the cross by the power of the Holy Spirit. Help that is real and effective, and not merely theoretical or theological, for multitudes who are wounded in body, soul and spirit.'

– John Arnott, Senior Pastor
Toronto Airport Christian Fellowship

'Here is essential reading for those who want to keep the renewal movement running on a true biblical basis. The book highlights the vital link between Calvary and Pentecost and is most timely and welcome.'

– Bishop David Pytches

'For too long the charismatic movement has fed on fast food. But of late we've got the taste for more substance. This book is the solid, real, gourmet cuisine we have longed for. Feast and enjoy. Then serve up the meal for others.'

– J. John

'It is rare to read a book that triggers moments of delighted recognition, "Yes, of course, that's it." In every section Mark Stibbe has managed to express what I know intuitively but never put into words. A sparkling work. Buy it and enjoy!'

– Eric Delve

'Full of fresh insights and vital reminders, Mark's book on the cross and the Spirit is a valuable teaching for the church.'

– Matt Redman

The Rev. Dr Mark Stibbe is Vicar of St Andrew's, Chorleywood. He is a popular speaker and author of many books including *Thinking Clearly about Revival* (Monarch). He and his wife Alie have four children.

Other books by Mark Stibbe:
John as Storyteller
John: A Readings Commentary
A Kingdom of Priests
Times of Refreshing
John's Gospel
The Gospel of John as Literature (edited)
O Brave New Church
Explaining Baptism in the Holy Spirit
Know Your Spiritual Gifts
Thinking Clearly about Revival
From Orphans to Heirs

Fire and Blood

The Work of the Spirit
The Work of the Cross

MARK STIBBE

MONARCH
BOOKS

First published by Monarch Books 2001

ISBN 1 85424 507 4

Unless otherwise stated, Scripture quotations are
taken from the Holy Bible, New International Version,
© 1973, 1978, 1984 by the International Bible Society.
Used by permission of Hodder & Stoughton Ltd.
All rights reserved.

British Library Cataloguing Data
A catalogue record for this book is available
from the British Library.

Designed and produced for the publishers by
Bookprint Creative Services
P.O. Box 827, BN21 3YJ, England.
Printed in Great Britain.

In affectionate memory of John Wimber –
a man of the cross and the Spirit

CONTENTS

ACKNOWLEDGEMENTS

There are many people I want to thank for their help in the writing of this book.

Thank you to the people of St Mark's, Grenoside, Sheffield, where I was vicar from January 1993 until January 1997. I first delivered parts of this book in a series of Lent addresses there in 1996. The response of the people there was extremely helpful.

Thank you to the people of Orebro Seminary in Sweden. I spent three weeks in that college lecturing on the cross and the Spirit during November and December 1996. I learnt many things from the interaction with the students during these classes.

Thank you to the people of St Andrew's, Chorleywood and Christ Church, Wimbledon who came with the Reverend Celia Thompson and me to watch the Oberammergau passion play this year. Some of what I have written here was delivered in the form of thirty-minute addresses in the ministry meetings in our hotel during that relaxing week. I am extremely grateful for the very positive feedback from the tour group about this material.

I want to thank Chris Mungeam at Sovereign World for his support, generosity and kindness.

Thanks too to the Reverend Michael Benjamin, for passing on to me a copy of Andrew Murray's priceless but neglected gem, *The Cross of Christ*.

Thanks also to John Hellewell, for letting me have a copy of his unpublished, informative MA dissertation on the relationship between the Spirit and the cross in the theology of Jurgen Moltmann (submitted in 1994 at St John's Theological College, Nottingham).

I want to thank those whose influence—acknowledged or not—lies somewhere behind this book. I am particularly grateful for the fact that I had a year training at St John's Nottingham under Tom Smail, whose writing and teaching on the cross has been an inspiration to many of us over the last two or three decades. Tom is one of the very few people who has looked at the relationship between the Spirit and the cross.

I want to express my debt to the late John Wimber, to whom this book is dedicated. John has had more impact on the churches in the UK than anyone else in recent times. He was the first person who taught me how to integrate evangelical and charismatic beliefs and practice. I could not have written this book without John's example and teaching. He was truly a man who shared in the fellowship of Christ's sufferings and ministered in the power of the Spirit.

Finally, I am very grateful to those who have taken the trouble to read the manuscript of this book so thoroughly. First and foremost, I want to thank my wife Alie, who has offered many helpful insights, especially in the sections on Hans Nielsen Hauge.

I want also to thank my dear friend Michael McCrum, who went through this book with a fine-tooth comb.

Many thanks to all of you.

Mark Stibbe,
August 2000

INTRODUCTION

'No eye has seen,
no ear has heard,
no mind has conceived
what God has prepared for those who love him' –
but God has revealed it to us by his Spirit.

1 Corinthians 2:9-10

A Christian theology of the Cross must be a Charismatic theology – one that depends on the Spirit's coming and the Spirit's working most of all.[1]

Tom Smail, *Once and For All. A Confession of the Cross*

When William Booth started the Salvation Army, he determined that its members should 'carry the Blood of Christ and the Fire of the Holy Ghost into every corner of the world'. Thereafter, the motto 'Blood and Fire' became increasingly popular and was the rallying cry of the membership.

In one brief phrase General William Booth managed to capture the theme of this entire book – the integration of the work of the cross and the work of the Spirit.

Today there are evangelicals who have a discipleship of the cross but who lack any real openness to the fire of the Holy Spirit. At the same time, there are others who are extremely open to the empowering presence of God but who lack any radical commitment to taking up their cross daily. One group stresses holiness. The other stresses healing. One group prays, 'more of the cross'. The other, 'more power'.

Andrew Murray once put it this way: 'Some cling to the cross and know not the power they may wait for there, and some seek the power and know not that at the cross it must be waited for.'[2]

It is my personal conviction that Jesus of Nazareth lived a dynamic life of weakness and wonders, suffering and glory. The future of biblical Christianity lies in recapturing this divine alliance of opposites in our own kingdom living. Unless we are apprehended by a vision for this potent paradox of the blood of Christ and the fire of the Spirit I do not believe we will make any real and lasting impact on the world around us. Indeed, I do not think that it is at all an exaggeration to say that the health of the contemporary church depends on it.

A charismatic approach

This book is subtitled 'The work of the Spirit, the work of the cross'. My approach to the cross is a charismatic one. What do I mean by 'charismatic'? The hallmark of charismatic spirituality is the belief that the gift and the gifts of the Spirit can be received as an experiential reality today. Charismatics believe that the same spiritual power that energised Jesus and the earliest Christians can inspire and empower us as well. Charismatics accordingly teach that all believers are to be baptised or 'drenched' in the power of the Holy Spirit, and continuously filled thereafter. We also teach that the gifts of the Holy Spirit – such as speaking in tongues, healing, miracles and prophecy – did not cease with the apostles but are still manifested today. Charismatic believers desire to see the kingdom of God extended through authoritative preaching and mighty works.

At the very core of charismatic spirituality is therefore an emphasis on the supernatural dimension to the Christian faith, and this is the distinctive characteristic of this book on the cross. What I am specifically interested in is the relationship between the work of the Spirit and the work of the cross. Part One has to do with the cross as it relates to Jesus Christ. Part Two has to do with the cross as it relates to the Christian.

The first chapter, 'Revelation and Redemption', examines the way in which the Holy Spirit prepared for the cross of Christ through the visions of the prophets and the sacrifices performed in the Temple.

The second chapter, 'Anointing and Affliction', looks at the work of the Spirit during the passion and death of Jesus. Here we ask the fascinating question, 'Where was the Holy Spirit at Calvary?'

In the third chapter, 'Passover and Pentecost', we see how the cross of Christ leads to the outpouring of the Spirit. Putting it crudely, we will see how Jesus had to be lifted up in order for the fire to come down.

In Part Two, we examine the relationship between the cross and the Spirit in the life of the believer. Here the emphasis is more on the cross in our *experience* rather than the cross as an *event*.

In chapter 4 we examine the relationship between 'Fullness and Faith'. We will see how a person can only enter salvation when the Holy Spirit applies the work of the cross to our lives.

In chapter 5 we explore the relationship between 'Mission and Miracles'. When the apostles sought to spread the message of Jesus they did so by preaching the cross with demonstrations of the Spirit's power.

This will take us, finally, to 'Brilliance and Brokenness'. Here we will look at the different ways in which the Holy Spirit draws us into closer fellowship with the cross.

Why have I divided the book this way? The New Testament describes the cross from two perspectives. It portrays the cross *objectively* (as a fact in history), and *subjectively* (as something in which we have to participate). In the first, the cross is an *event* in the past. In the second, the cross is an *experience* in our present. Both of these aspects are joined together in 1 Peter 2:24, where the apostle writes of Jesus: 'He himself bore our sins in his body on the tree, so that we might die to sins and live for righteousness.'

Peter deals first with the fact of the cross, secondly with the fellowship of the cross. The first stresses Christ's death *for* us. The second Christ's death *in* us. I will do the same in this book.

The reasons for this book

There are a number of reasons why I felt moved to write this book.

First of all, there has been a great neglect of the relationship between the Spirit and the cross in theology generally. In recent decades there has been a considerable amount of work on the cross by theologians who would not call themselves either pentecostal or charismatic. The name

Jurgen Moltmann is perhaps the most famous associated with these new studies. However, while Moltmann and others give considerable attention to the work of the Father and the Son at Calvary, he gives far less space to the work of the Spirit.[3] This gap has needed filling and, even though I would not claim that this book is an example of academic theology (certainly not at the level Moltmann operates), it is an attempt to complete the picture.

Secondly, the cross has suffered neglect by charismatics. Indeed, charismatics have a reputation for being forgetful of the cross (a reputation that is actually less fair than is realised). I well remember writing a popular, theological book on what the British media described as 'the Toronto Blessing'.[4] This resulted in some fairly aggressive letters being written, one of which accused me of totally omitting any concern for the cross. The writer asked how I could write a whole book about the Holy Spirit without a single reference to Calvary. In actual fact, there were over twenty direct references to the cross and quite a number of implied references too. Nevertheless, the comments hit home. I had already completed a course of lectures on the relationship between the Spirit and the cross. I had also begun to put these thoughts down on paper. So I vowed there and then that this book would one day be written.

A third major reason why I have written this book has to do with revival. Many of us are longing, praying and working towards a revival of authentic, biblical Christianity in our community and nation. But do we realise that we will never have revival while the Spirit and the cross remain separated? There can be no genuine revival among believers unless we seek the cross-shaped life. There can be no genuine revival among unbelievers unless we are prepared to preach Christ crucified with demonstrations of the Spirit's power. Revival can therefore only occur in churches where the work of the Spirit and the work of the cross are not divorced but united in a rich and life-giving marriage. As William Booth saw, we need the fire and the blood together.

I began this brief introduction with a quotation from Andrew Murray. I will end it with one. 'If the teaching of the church is to be full and fruitful, if it is to be the channel and the bearer of God's mighty saving power, it must, above everything, know and show the intimate union between the cross and the Spirit.'[5]

That, in brief, is the subject of this book.

Part One

The Life of Jesus

PROLOGUE

There was a long queue leading to the river's edge. And what a motley crowd of people stood there! Some of the women were prostitutes. Others were housewives and mothers. Some of the men were rough, violent types. Others were well-to-do businessmen. All sorts. Even the occasional priest, with the give-away prayer shawl over his head and shoulders.

Yet they were all joined by one common bond, a desire to go to the river and get right with God.

They had heard about John the Baptist. Who hadn't? His was a household name in Judea. Everyone knew about him. How he had taken a Nazarite vow, how his lips had never touched alcohol, how he ate the most unusual diet, how he had laid into the religious hypocrites from Jerusalem, and how his hair had grown long and unkempt. Everyone knew his story. But what drew them to the waters was far more than just a desire to come face to face with a well-known, eccentric personality. There was something deeper than that, for this man was on a mission from God. This man was a torchbearer for holiness. While the moneymakers were saying 'Earn', and the teachers of the law were saying 'Learn', John was saying, 'Turn!' And people queued up in the process to hear they were sinners!

But there was one man in the line that day who was not a sinner. He stood with thieves and swindlers, ruthless tax collectors and corrupt priests, loose-living women and men with sexually transmitted diseases. His name, in the language of his culture, was *Yeshua*, meaning 'salvation'. We know him as 'Jesus'.

Jesus was also on a mission from God, though not the same as John's. John's mandate was to prepare the way. Jesus' mandate was to BE the way. John's mandate was to be a voice in the wilderness. Jesus' was to be the word. John's mandate was to be the best man. Jesus' to be the bridegroom. John's mandate was to be a lamp burning brightly for a while. Jesus' was to be the light of the world. John's mandate was to plunge people in water. Jesus' to plunge them in the Holy Spirit.

As the queue formed at the river, the sinners were joined by one who was without sin. Mortal men and women rubbed shoulders with the eternal Son of God. Lowly subjects waited in line with the king of kings.

And as they did so, John looked up and saw Jesus of Nazareth.

It was said that John had been filled with the *ruach ha kodesh* – the Holy Spirit – even from his birth. Today he felt the pressure of divine intuition as never before as he looked at the man in the crowd. Jesus of Nazareth had no great looks nor did he wear royal robes. But to the eye of the last of the old covenant prophets this man appeared altogether different. Straight away John knew who he was. Turning from the man he had just baptised, he fixed his eyes on Jesus. Under the strongest anointing he had ever known, he declared, 'Behold, the Lamb of God, who takes away the sin of the world.'

Everyone stopped in their tracks. People whispered to each other. 'Who does he mean?' 'What's he talking about?'

Then Jesus stepped forward, walking right up to John –
waist high in the Jordan river.

As John baptised him, he saw the Spirit of God descend
from an open heaven in the form of a dove, alighting and
remaining on the person of Jesus. Earlier on the Holy Spirit
had revealed to John that a man would come to him and
the Spirit would descend upon him and *remain* on him.
This man would be the one who would put an end to the
long drought of the Spirit in Israel.

And so, on that momentous day, John's destiny was fulfilled. The one he had spent his life preparing for and
preaching about had at last come.

The Lamb who was to take away the sin of the world,
and the one on whom the dove of God's Spirit remained.
The man of the cross, man of the Spirit.

Chapter 1

REVELATION AND REDEMPTION

Concerning this salvation, the prophets, who spoke of the grace that was to come to you, searched intently and with the greatest care, trying to find out the time and circumstances to which the Spirit of Christ in them was pointing when he predicted the sufferings of Christ and the glories that would follow.

1 Peter 1:10–11

The highest point of revelation occurred in the deepest pit of human tragedy – a crucifixion.[1]

George Eldon Ladd

Not long ago I visited the southernmost tip of Norway and stood on a high rock overlooking the sea. It was a bright day with perfect visibility. On my left was Lindesnes lighthouse, on my right high cliffs leading further along the coast. I had climbed to a high vantage point overlooking the North Sea and was now peering through a powerful

telescope at the waves that rose and fell in the clear mid-
day sun.

The thing I remember most vividly was the effect of the
wind. It was so strong and it had come suddenly. As my
family and I drove towards Lindesnes, there had been no
sign of it, though the tall wind-driven propellers near the
coast might have alerted us. During our approach the air
was still, the temperature hot and the weather perfect. As
we parked our car and got out, we all became aware of a
stronger breeze. Nothing, however, prepared us for the
power of the wind on the top of the cliffs. As we climbed
to the summit, we were hit by it very suddenly as we came
out of the shelter of the rocks. It was so strong that the children were barely able to stand.

Looking through the telescope I witnessed a wonderful
sight. I had not expected to see anything other than the
occasional oil tanker slowly moving through the ranks of
'white horses'. But moving from right to left as I looked a
tall ship in beautiful condition was sailing at some speed.
Its large, white canvas sails were filled like bursting chests
with the mighty wind that was blowing. It was a magnificent spectacle. A large sailing ship was being carried along
by the wind and the waves, its crew of seafarers – no doubt
filled with the bravado of their Viking ancestors – working
hard to harness the raw power of nature.

The Spirit of God

Think of the wind and you can think of the Spirit of God.
In fact, the Hebrew word for Spirit is *ruach*, which can also
be translated 'wind'. We find this word used 377 times in
the Hebrew Scriptures (the Old Testament). On 115 occasions it means 'wind' or 'air'. Thus we read how God sent
a much needed wind at the time of the flood: 'But God

remembered Noah and all the wild animals and the live-stock that were with him in the ark, and he sent a wind [*ruach*] over the earth, and the waters receded' (Genesis 8:1). On 100 occasions it means God's Spirit. Genesis 1:2 says: 'Now the earth was formless and empty, darkness was over the surface of the deep, and the Spirit [*ruach*] of God was hovering over the waters.'

What a perfect image for describing the Holy Spirit. Like the wind, you cannot actually see the Holy Spirit, only the signs of his presence. When a tree is shaken by the wind, you cannot see the wind itself but you can see its effects. Thus the prophet Isaiah says, 'Now the house of David was told, "Aram has allied itself with Ephraim"; so the hearts of Ahaz and his people were shaken, as the trees of the forest are shaken by the wind [*ruach*]' (Isaiah 7:2).

So it is with the Holy Spirit. We are aware of his manifest presence by virtue of its effects. The Spirit himself is, how-ever, incorporeal and intangible. He has no physical body and you cannot touch him (although his effects can be seen in physical bodies and he can certainly touch us).

Like the wind, there are varying levels of the Spirit's presence. The word *ruach* can be translated 'breeze' or it can be translated 'tempest'. In Genesis 3:8 we read how God walked in the garden in the cool (*ruach*) of the day. Here the word refers to a calm, refreshing wind. However, in Psalm 55 verse 8, after David has longed for the wings of a dove, the same word is translated as a 'tempest'. He exclaims, 'I would hurry to my place of shelter, far from the tempest [*ruach*] and storm.' Like the wind, the Spirit of God can move with a power that varies from Force 1 to Force 9.

Like the wind, the ways of the Spirit are also mysterious. Thus we find the Lord Jesus speaking of the sovereign tra-jectories of the Spirit using the imagery of the wind. He spoke in Aramaic, but our Greek New Testaments still preserve the *double entendre*. In Greek, *ruach* is rendered *pneuma*, and *pneuma* can also be translated as either wind or Spirit: 'The wind [*pneuma*] blows wherever it pleases. You hear its sound, but you cannot tell where it comes from or where it is going. So it is with everyone born of the Spirit' (John 3:8).

Like the wind, finally, the Spirit proceeds from God. The source of the Holy Spirit is not in humanity nor in nature but in God. The prophet Jeremiah says, '[God] sends lightning with the rain and brings out the wind from his storehouses' (Jeremiah 10:13). Just as the wind comes from God, so does the Spirit. The Spirit is the Spirit *of God*, or the Spirit *of the Lord*. When God promises to visit his people in supernatural power, he says, 'I will pour out *my* Spirit on all people' (Joel 2:28). Just as God sends the wind out of his storehouses, so he sends the Holy Spirit. Just as the wind goes out from the Lord (Numbers 11:31), so the Spirit proceeds from God himself.

This brings us to the most important fact about the Holy Spirit, his relationship to the Godhead. The one weakness of the word 'wind' is its impersonal connotation. Wind is air in motion. It is not a person. Yet the Bible as a whole reveals that the Holy Spirit is personal not impersonal. The Holy Spirit is not just an aspect of God, as the phrase 'Spirit of the Lord' might imply. He is a divine person in his own right. Thus, when Jesus speaks about the Holy Spirit, he uses a noun that is neuter (*pneuma*) but follows it with a pronoun that is masculine (*ekeinos*): 'When he, the Spirit [*pneuma*] of truth comes, he [*ekeinos*] will guide you into all truth' (John 16:13). While images such as wind, fire, water and oil are helpful in suggesting the *work* of the Spirit, they have limited value in describing the *nature* of the Spirit. The Spirit is a divine person, not an impersonal force.

Right from the beginning of the Bible we receive hints that the Godhead is a community of persons in one being. In Genesis 1:26 God says, 'Let *us* make man in *our* image' (my italics). In Isaiah 6:8, God says, 'Whom shall I send? And who will go for *us*?' (my italics). However, it was not until the coming of Jesus that a fuller picture begins to emerge. In the pages of the New Testament we learn that God is one divine essence or being, eternally existing in three persons – Father, Son and Holy Spirit. In this respect, the words of the risen Jesus to his disciples are of critical importance: 'Therefore go and make disciples of all nations, baptising them *in the name of the Father and of the Son and of the Holy Spirit*' (Matthew 28:19, my italics). The Apostle Paul also points to the triunity of God: 'May the grace of the Lord Jesus Christ, and the love of God, and the fellowship of the Holy Spirit be with you all' (2 Corinthians 13:14). Here again, God is one in three and three in one.

He has spoken by the prophets

The story of the Bible is the story of how the triune God has chosen to reveal himself and make himself known to his people. Throughout the Old Testament, the Spirit of God comes and goes like the wind, anointing this person, then another, always obeying the Father's bidding and pointing beyond himself to the Son who is to come into the world as Saviour. True prophecy is therefore a trinitarian event: the Father sends his Spirit to reveal his Son. As the writer to the Hebrews puts it, 'In the past God spoke to our forefathers through the prophets at many times and in various ways' (Hebrews 1:1).

It has never been in the nature of the Spirit to draw attention to himself. It is his passion and delight to glorify the Son. When I was looking through the telescope on the cliffs of Lindesnes, it was not so much the wind that I noticed as the boat whose sails the wind was filling. So it is with the Holy Spirit. It is not his longing that we should stand in awe of him; rather that we should marvel at the one to whom he has always pointed, the one whom he filled without measure, the one whom he now glorifies – the Son of God.

During the Old Testament era, the Holy Spirit spoke primarily through the prophets. The prophets were men of the Spirit. In fact, the Apostle Peter states that these men were 'carried along' by the Spirit: 'You must understand that no prophecy of Scripture came about by the prophet's own interpretation. For prophecy never had its origin in the will of man, but men spoke from God as they were carried along by the Holy Spirit' (2 Peter 1:20–21).

The verb 'carried along' is fascinating here. In Greek it is *pherein*. This word is used twice in the famous story of Paul's shipwreck in Acts 27:

> The ship was caught by the storm and could not head into the wind; so we gave way to it and were driven along [*pherein*]. As we passed to the lee of a small island called Cauda, we were hardly able to make the lifeboat secure. When the men had hoisted it aboard, they passed ropes under the ship itself to hold it together. Fearing that they would run aground on the sandbars of Syrtis, they lowered the sea anchor and let the ship be driven along [*pherein*].
>
> Acts 27:15–17

Just as Paul's ship was carried along by the wind, so the prophets of the Old Testament were carried along by the Spirit. Their words did not originate in the will of man but in the will of God.

All this has major implications for our understanding of

the relationship between the work of the Spirit and the event of the cross. Throughout the Old Testament, God was revealing his secret plan of salvation to the prophets through the power of his Spirit. That this included the Calvary event is made very evident in another passage in the writings of the Apostle Peter:

> Concerning this salvation, the prophets, who spoke of the grace that was to come to you, searched intently and with the greatest care, trying to find out the time and circumstances to which the Spirit of Christ in them was pointing when he predicted the sufferings of Christ and the glories that would follow.
>
> 1 Peter 1:10–11

Here Peter explicitly states that the source of revelation in the prophets was the Spirit of Christ. The Spirit who anointed and remained upon the Messiah Jesus was also at work 'in' or 'with' the prophets. His ministry was to show them a vision of what was to come, specifically the suffering of the Messiah, and the glorious events that followed (the exaltation of Jesus).

In another New Testament passage, we learn that the Holy Spirit was also at work in the old covenant sacrifices, initially performed in the Tabernacle, and then subsequently in the Temple. Every time an animal was put to death as an atonement for sin, the Holy Spirit was showing God's people that there was something superior to come, namely the cross of Christ. The same verb is used here in Hebrews 9:8 as in 1 Peter 1:11 – *deluein*: 'to show', 'to reveal', 'to declare'. Both prophets and priests were carried along by the Spirit, speaking and acting so as to reveal the 'once and for all' sacrifice of God's Son.

Truly, the Spirit was leading to the cross.

The suffering servant

No prophet saw these things more clearly than Isaiah. Isaiah's ministry began with a vision of God 'high and lifted up' (Isaiah 6:1,KJV). It was 740 BC, the year that King Uzziah died. As Isaiah was in the Temple, he saw the holiness of God and wept on account of his own unholiness. An angel administered cleansing, and Isaiah received a call to go to the nation of Israel with a warning of the coming judgement of God. Subsequent chapters describe God's anger against Israel and the nations. They also reveal a sign of hope, the coming of Immanuel, 'God with us'. Later, in chapters 40-55, this person is described as the servant of *Yahweh*.

There are four passages that describe this servant of God, but the fourth (Isaiah 52:13 – 53:12) is the most remarkable. Here the Spirit of Christ can be seen at work in the prophet Isaiah. Isaiah sees a servant who will be 'raised and lifted up' (52:13). This is exactly the language that Isaiah uses of God in 6:1. The servant is therefore Immanuel, God with us on the earth. However, what comes next is a surprise. This divine servant will not appear as a victor but as a victim. Though the servant will be full of wisdom (a mark of the Spirit – Isaiah 11:2), he will suffer a cruel death. He will be so disfigured that people will cry out, 'Is this a human being?' (52:14). Yet through his sufferings, many will be sprinkled with his blood and find atonement and salvation (52:15).

How is this servant going to suffer? Though this man is 'the arm of the Lord' (ie God Almighty [53:1]), he will grow up before God as a human being. His growth will be natural, 'like a tender shoot, and like a root out of dry ground' (53:2). There will be nothing special about his appearance. He will not look like a majestic king (53:2). He

will be despised and rejected, a man of sorrows, one familiar with suffering. Far from looking at him with admiration, people will turn their faces away in disgust (53:3). He
will be pierced, crushed and wounded (53:5). He will be
led to his death like the silent lamb of the Passover sacrifices (53:7). He will be the victim of criminal injustice. He
will be cut off in his youth, leaving no family. He will die
violently, like a branch being hacked from a tree (53:8). He
will be buried in a rich man's grave (53:9). But this will not
be the end. There are glories to follow these sufferings.
Even though he dies, he will be made alive again and will
be delighted by the benefits won for many by his death
(53:10–11).

Why is this servant going to suffer? In order to die in our
place. Everything in these verses points to a substitutionary death. The purpose of the servant's suffering will be to
bear our sins. He will take the burden of our sufferings and
sorrows and carry them on his shoulders. He will be tortured and killed because of our wilful disobedience and
our inherent rebellion, but through the blows he receives
there will be *shalom* or peace. There will be healing for our
spirits, souls and bodies (53:5). Though we have turned
away from God like wandering sheep, the servant will
bear the consequences of our actions (53:6). He will volun-
tarily submit himself to the will of God and fulfil the role
of substitute (53:7–8) and his sinlessness will make this
substitution acceptable to God as a guilt offering (53:9–10).

The miracle of prophecy

Could there be a more remarkable prophecy than this?
With astonishing accuracy, the prophet Isaiah foresaw the
sufferings of Christ and the glories that were to follow. In
fact, almost every detail in Isaiah's vision is fulfilled in

Jesus. Consider the part of Isaiah 53 that relates to the suffering and death of the servant (vv 3–7,9) and you will see how true this is. If we put the name of Jesus as the subject of the statements, it becomes clear how much of the Calvary event fulfils what Isaiah foresaw:

[Jesus] was despised and rejected by men,
A man of sorrows, and familiar with suffering.
Like one from whom men hide their faces
He was despised, and we esteemed him not.

Surely [Jesus] took up our infirmities
And carried our sorrows,
Yet we considered him stricken by God,
Smitten by him, and afflicted.

But [Jesus] was pierced for our transgressions,
He was crushed for our iniquities;
The punishment that brought us peace was upon him,
And by his wounds we are healed.

We all, like sheep, have gone astray,
Each of us has turned to his own way;
And the Lord has laid on [Jesus]
The iniquity of us all.

[Jesus] was oppressed and afflicted,
Yet he did not open his mouth;
He was led like a lamb to the slaughter,
And as a sheep before her shearers is silent,
So he did not open his mouth.

[Jesus] was assigned a grave with the wicked,
And with the rich in his death,
Though he had done no violence,
Nor was any deceit in his mouth.

How is that Isaiah could foresee the cross with such accuracy? The clue is in Isaiah 53:1 – 'Who has believed our message and to whom has the arm of the Lord been *revealed*?' The word 'revealed' shows that this vision is the result of prophetic revelation, not human speculation. At some point in his life, Isaiah was carried along by the Holy Spirit and saw a vision of the death, burial and resurrection of the Messiah.

It is for this reason that the Apostle Peter can apply the details of the fourth servant song to the death of Jesus in his first letter. Having just spoken of the way the Spirit leads to the cross, Peter then proves the point by describing the death of Jesus using the language of Isaiah 53: 'You know that it was not with perishable things such as silver or gold that you were redeemed from the empty way of life handed down to you from your forefathers, but with the precious blood of Christ, *a lamb without blemish or defect*' (1 Peter 1:18–19, my italics). And again:

> To this you were called, because Christ suffered for you, leaving you an example, that you should follow in his steps. *'He committed no sin, and no deceit was found in his mouth.'* When they hurled their insults at him, he did not retaliate; when he suffered, he made no threats. Instead, he entrusted himself to him who judges justly. *He himself bore our sins* in his body on the tree, so that we might die to sins and live for righteousness; *by his wounds you have been healed*. For you were *like sheep going astray*, but now you have returned to the Shepherd and Overseer of your souls.
>
> 1 Peter 2:21–25, my italics

Peter can do this because Isaiah was empowered by the Holy Spirit to speak of the circumstances of our salvation and the time of the grace that was to come.

All this should fill us with wonder. In his first sermon, Peter said this to the crowds gathered in Jerusalem: 'This man [Jesus] was handed over to you by God's set purpose and foreknowledge; and you, with the help of wicked men, put him to death by nailing him to the cross' (Acts 2:23).

Peter knew that the passion and death of Jesus had been part of the Father's plan. He understood by revelation of the Holy Spirit that both the cross and the resurrection had been foretold in Scripture and this alone was evidence of God's sovereignty. As he was later to say in his first letter, he knew that the Spirit of Christ had forewarned the prophets concerning the sufferings of Christ and the glories that were to follow.

In the light of all this, we have to conclude that Old Testament prophecy comes under the category of the miraculous. Only by the inspiration of the Holy Spirit could the prophets have seen the birth, life, death and resurrection of Jesus with such accuracy. It has been estimated that there are 330 messianic prophecies in the Old Testament which have been fulfilled in Jesus. Using the science of probability, Professor Peter Stoner has estimated that the chances of just eight of these being fulfilled in the life of just one man is 1 in 10^{17}. That would be 1 in 100,000,000,000,000,000! To help us comprehend the nature of this probability, Professor Stoner uses a vivid and striking analogy:

Suppose we take 10^{17} silver dollars and lay them down on the face of Texas. They will cover all the state two feet deep. Now mark one of these silver dollars and stir the whole mass thoroughly, all over the state. Blindfold a man and tell him that he can travel as far as he wishes, but he must pick up one silver dollar and say this is the right one. What chance would he have of getting the right one? Just the same chance that the prophets would have had of writing these eight prophecies and having them all come true in any one man.[2]

Here, then, is the miracle of prophecy. During the old covenant era, the Holy Spirit used the sacrificial system to point to the superior way of atonement provided at Calvary. At the same time, the Holy Spirit spoke through prophets like Isaiah concerning the suffering servant. As Alfred Edersheim puts it, 'In Christ alone these two ideas of the Paschal Lamb and the Righteous Suffering Servant of Jehovah are combined into a unity'.[3] The probability of just these two being fulfilled in one man is massive.

The mystery of prophecy

Yet, not everyone agrees with this thesis. Many Jewish scholars today claim that Isaiah 53 has never been regarded as a prophecy of the Messiah by their own people, and certainly not before the time of Jesus. Indeed, they go further than this, stating that Isaiah's vision of the suffering servant does not refer to an individual messianic figure but refers to the people of Israel as a whole, suffering oppression and affliction throughout their troubled history. In his book, *You Take Jesus, I'll Take God*, Samuel Levine gives voice to the common Jewish view concerning Isaiah 53:

> Many Jewish commentators feel that it refers to the Jewish people as a whole. We find many instances in the Bible where the Jewish people on the whole are addressed, or are described, in the singular. . . . Thus, Isaiah 53 could very well be describing the history of the Jewish people – despised by the world, persecuted by the crusaders and the Spanish Inquisition and the Nazis, while the world silently watched. The verses therefore do not point exclusively to Jesus, or to a Messiah. . . .[4]

No one can deny that the people of Israel have endured the most appalling persecution, not least at the hands of the church during the last two millennia. This should be a matter of intense grief to all Christian believers, so we must take care not to give pat answers. Having said that, we need to make a response to the two standard Jewish claims that Isaiah 53 refers to Israel not the Messiah, and that Isaiah 53 has therefore never been interpreted as a prophecy of the Messiah.

First of all, let us deal very quickly with the view that the suffering servant refers to Israel not an individual. This is very questionable. Isaiah says, 'for the transgression of *my people* he was stricken' (Isaiah 53:8, my italics). How can the suffering servant be stricken for God's people and at the same time *be* God's people? That makes no sense at all. Furthermore, Isaiah stresses that the suffering servant was a person without violence and deceit and who was righteous. This is not true of the people of Israel as a whole. Their history is punctuated with sin, not least in the Old Testament era. It is therefore very hard to believe that the suffering servant in Isaiah 53 can refer to Israel.

Secondly, is it really true that the Jewish community has never interpreted the suffering servant of Isaiah 53 as a prophecy of the messiah? The answer to this is 'No'. Here are three reasons.

1. There is some evidence that the Dead Sea Scrolls contain a messianic interpretation of Isaiah 53. A fragment from Cave 4 has been found, six lines in length, which begins, 'Isaiah the Prophet.' It refers to a shoot springing from the stock of Jesse. This figure is also described as 'the Branch of David'. The next part of the text is very damaged and hard to translate, but some scholars believe that it portrays this figure being taken to court and killed 'by strokes and by wounds' (an allusion to Isaiah 53). Others, however, believe that the verb 'kill' (*hmtw*) is active, and that the Messiah is therefore doing the killing, not being killed. The verb can be translated both actively and passively. While

the jury is still out on a definite translation, the publication of this fragment (known rather blandly as 4Q 285, fragment 5) caused a sensation in 1991. The idea that there might have been a messianic interpretation of Isaiah 53 from a Jewish community prior to the time of Jesus was startling indeed.[5]

2. Messianic Jews with a great knowledge of the Targums, the Talmud and the Mishnah have looked again at these texts to check whether it really is true that Isaiah 53 has not been interpreted as messianic prophecy. The findings have been very revealing. They have discovered that in fact there is good evidence from ancient rabbinical sources that the suffering servant of Isaiah 53 was interpreted as the Messiah, and that the view that this servant was Israel was not seriously proposed until the eleventh century. The following are just a few examples:[6]

a) The Targum (ancient translation) of the Book of Isaiah says this of Isaiah 53: 'Behold, my Servant the Messiah shall prosper. . . . All of us were scattered like sheep. . . . but it is the will of God to pardon the sins of all of us on his account. . . . Because he was ready to suffer martyrdom.'

b) The Babylonian Talmud contains commentaries on Isaiah 53, one of which says, 'God will burden the Messiah with commandments and sufferings as with millstones' (Talmud Sanhedrin 93b). Another passage in the same book discusses what name should be given to the Messiah. The disciples of the school of Rabbi Yehuda Ha'Nasi say he should be called 'The sick one', for it is written, 'Surely he has borne our sicknesses, etc.' (Talmud Sanhedrin 98 b).

c) The Midrash of Isaiah 53. One Rabbi cites the views of another Rabbi: 'The sufferings are divided into three parts: one for David and the fathers, one for our own generation, and one for King Messiah, and this is what is written, "He was wounded for our transgressions." In another part of the Midrash, called the Haggadah, the Holy One (God) makes an agreement with the Messiah and says to him, 'The sins of those which are forgiven for your sake will cause you to be put under an iron yoke. . . . And on account of their sins your tongue shall cleave to your mouth' (Pesiqta Rabbati, chapter 36). In the next chapter, the sufferings of Isaiah 53 are attributed to 'our Righteous Messiah'.

Though some of these may derive from a period after the New Testament era, they undoubtedly reflect and preserve oral teachings that go back to the time of Jesus and probably even further back. They show, after all, that some rabbis really did interpret the suffering servant as the Messiah.

3. There is evidence that at least one Hasidic group in contemporary Judaism is beginning to interpret Isaiah 53 in a messianic way. I am referring to the Lubavitch sect who regarded rabbi Menachem Mendel Schneerson as the Messiah. The rabbi, who died in 1994, was a remarkable person with a world-wide following of disciples. He succeeded in taking Torah Judaism to new people, in renewing Jewish education, and in leading countless irreligious Jews back into obedience to the Law. Thousands believed him to be the Messiah but he then suffered a stroke – a disqualification of messianic status in traditional Jewish thought. Undeterred, his disciples made the extraordinary move of claiming that the rabbi's illness was redemptive suffering, and that in this he was fulfilling the prophecy concerning the suffering servant of Isaiah 53! This willingness on the part of Hasidic Jews to believe that the Messiah could suffer and die has caused huge disturbance in the

Jewish world. After all, this is the main reason that Jews have rejected that Jesus might be the Messiah! As one rabbi has written, 'It is now conceded that the Messiah can die. The ground-rules for Jewish-Christian dialogue have been changed for ever.'[7] As another Jewish professor has written, 'Our children will no longer be able to tell Christian missionaries that the Jewish faith does not countenance belief in a Messiah whose mission is interrupted by death, and one of the defining characteristics of Judaism in a Christian world will have been erased.'[8]

The wrong packaging

Prophecies of Calvary were therefore in the Old Testament all the time, and there is at least some evidence that passages like Psalm 22 and Isaiah 53 have been interpreted in a messianic way by Jewish people.

Jesus himself interpreted his mission in terms of Isaiah 53, and Jesus was very much a Jew of his day. He spoke Aramaic, not Latin. He was a rabbi, not a vicar. He wore a prayer shawl, not a dog collar. He worshipped at the synagogue, not a church. He made pilgrimage to Jerusalem, not to Rome. And he celebrated Passover, not Easter. Jesus was Jewish through and through. No one now doubts that Jesus was an Aramaic-speaking, *hasid* (holy man), whose teaching is best understood in terms of the Jewish culture of his day.

We must therefore take very seriously Jesus' own use of Isaiah 53 as the background to his own ministry. Indeed, Jesus, a Jewish rabbi, found no difficulty in seeing his impending death as a fulfilment of Isaiah 53: 'It is written: "And he was numbered with the transgressors"; and I tell you that this must be fulfilled in me. Yes, what is written about me is reaching its fulfilment' (Luke 22:37).

Having said all that, this view of the suffering Messiah

was not the dominant expectation of Jesus' day. Many Jewish people of the time were expecting a more triumphant messianic figure. Peter obviously had no room for the cross in his thinking (Matthew 16:22).The two disciples walking down the Emmaus Road were clearly surprised and devastated by the death of Jesus. Jesus therefore says: '"How foolish you are, and how slow of heart to believe all that the prophets have spoken! Did not the Christ have to suffer these things and then enter his glory?" And beginning with Moses and all the Prophets, he explained to them what was said in all the Scriptures concerning himself' (Luke 24:25–27).

Happily these two Jewish disciples were put right by what must have been the most fascinating Bible study of all time. But others were not so wise. What a sad thing it is when people miss the gift because of its packaging.

The story is told of a young man who was getting ready to graduate from college. For many months he had admired a beautiful sports car in a dealer's showroom, and knowing his father could well afford it, he told him that was all he wanted. As graduation day approached, the young man awaited signs that his father had purchased the car. Finally, on the morning of his graduation, his father called him into his private study.

His father told him how proud he was to have such a fine son, and told him how much he loved him. He handed his son a beautiful wrapped gift box. Curious, but somewhat disappointed, the young man opened the box and found a lovely, leather-bound Bible, with the young man's name embossed in gold. Angrily, he raised his voice to his father and said, 'With all your money you give me a Bible?' and stormed out of the house, leaving the Bible behind.

Many years passed and the young man was very successful in business. He had a beautiful home and wonderful family, but realised his father was very old, and thought perhaps he should go to him. He had not seen him since that graduation day.

Before he could make arrangements, he received a telegram telling him his father had passed away, and willed all of his possessions to his son. He needed to come home immediately and take care of things. When he arrived at his father's house, sudden sadness and regret filled his heart. He began to search through his father's important papers and saw the still new Bible, just as he had left it years ago.

With tears, he opened the Bible and began to turn the pages. His father had carefully underlined a verse, Matthew 7:11 (KJV): 'If ye, then, being evil, know how to give good gifts unto your children, how much more shall your Father which is in heaven, give good things to them that ask him?'

As he read those words, a car key dropped from the Bible. It had a tag with the dealer's name, the same dealer who had the sports car he had desired. On the tag was the date of his graduation, and the words: 'PAID IN FULL'.

It is a tragic thing that so many people in Israel at the time of Jesus missed the great gift of salvation because they could not cope with the packaging. It is a tragic thing that so many Jewish people still believe that Jesus cannot have been the Messiah because the Messiah was not supposed to suffer and die. Until they unwrap the present that the Father has already given, they – and all others like them – will never know that their sins have been 'paid in full'.

The mystery of salvation

Professor Geza Vermes is regarded as one of the leading Jewish scholars of the New Testament and the Jewish literature of the period. He has studied the secondary literature in great depth and concluded that Jews at the time of Jesus were not expecting a Messiah whose mission would be interrupted by suffering and death. He has written: 'Despite the availability of the Dead Sea Scrolls, the 19-centuries-old historical enigma of how the concept of a suffering and dying Messiah penetrated the New Testament remains as mysterious as ever.'[9]

The word to underline is 'mysterious'. From a human perspective, the idea of a crucified Messiah was a mystery to most Jewish people of Jesus' day. But looking at this subject at the human level is not enough. In his first letter to Corinth, the Apostle Paul states that the idea of a crucified Messiah could only have come by charismatic revelation. In other words, Paul is emphatic that such a vision could only have been revealed by the Holy Spirit. The idea that the Messiah would triumph through tragedy was simply too weak for any human philosopher to come up with. It was utter foolishness to the sophisticated mind (1 Corinthians 1:18). However, to the one whose mind is illuminated by the Holy Spirit, the cross of Christ was regarded as God's 'secret wisdom' (1 Corinthians 2:7) or 'mystery'. Thus, only the spiritual mind can receive the revelation of the depth and power of the cross (1 Corinthians 2:14). The Spirit alone unveils the hidden beauty of Calvary.

As we consider the mystery of salvation, it is important to remember that Paul regarded this as something hidden during the centuries prior to the coming of Jesus. He stresses, 'We speak of God's secret wisdom, a wisdom that has been hidden and that God destined for our glory before time began' (1 Corinthians 2:7). The reason it was hidden is that the Holy Spirit had departed from Israel. The rabbis believed that the Holy Spirit had ceased to be present in Israel after the last prophets, Haggai, Zechariah and Malachi, had died. It is therefore hardly surprising to find so few rabbis writing about a suffering Messiah in the Second Temple period. Though the seeds of this vision were certainly already in Scripture, they could only be cultivated into a coherent messianic expectation through the work of the Spirit.

The point is this: only a person with a very distinct and strong prophetic call was going to discern that God would redeem his people through a Roman cross. In spite of the Old Testament preparation, this was truly a tale of the unexpected; truly an example of the God of surprises at work. Only a person with eyes to see what the Spirit of God was doing would be able to fathom such a mystery. Only one who flew on eagle's wings to the highest levels of divine wisdom would be able to know such holy secrets. As George Eldon Ladd once put it, 'The highest point of revelation occurred in the deepest pit of human tragedy – a crucifixion.' It takes a genuine prophet to see that!

Behold the Lamb of God

John the Baptist was such a man. He was the last of the Old Testament prophets, filled with the Holy Spirit even from birth. Seeing Jesus of Nazareth approaching the River Jordan, John declared him to be the Lamb of God who takes away the sin of the world (John 1:29). By charismatic revelation John saw that Jesus was the substitutionary lamb foreseen by Isaiah and the fulfilment of the messianic hopes of Passover. The way Jesus dies gives ample evidence that John was right. Note the following facts:

1. The innocence of Jesus

Pilate insists that he can find no basis for a charge against

Jesus (John 19:4,6). In other words, Pilate emphasises Jesus' innocence. This detail is important because one of the requirements for the Passover lamb was that it should be male, one year old, and without defect (Exodus 12:5). Jesus is declared to be 'without defect' by Pilate.

2. The branch of hyssop

When Jesus was hanging on the cross, John reports that a soldier lifted a sponge soaked in wine vinegar to Jesus' lips, and that he used a branch of hyssop to do this (John 19:29). In Exodus 12:22, the Lord commands his people to take a bunch of hyssop, dip it in the blood of the Passover lamb, and then daub it on the top and both sides of the door-frames of their houses in Egypt. When the angel of death came to Egypt, he would pass over those homes covered by the blood of the lambs, and the firstborn sons in those houses would be spared. The hyssop branch used at the cross reinforces the connection between the death of Jesus and the slaughter of the Passover lambs.

3. The day of Preparation

Three times John stresses that Jesus died on this day (John 19:14,31,42). This was the day on which the fathers of each household took a one-year-old male lamb to the Temple precincts to be slaughtered. In the Mishnah, we read an account of what actually happened in the period before the Temple was destroyed by the Romans in AD 70: 'An Israelite slaughtered his own offering and the priest caught the blood. The priest passed the basin to his fellow, and he to his fellow, each receiving a full basin and giving back an empty one. The priest nearest the altar tossed the blood in one action against the base.' In John 19, Jesus dies when the lambs are being put to death in the Temple courts. At the moment when fathers were leading lambs to the slaughter, Jesus went to the cross to die as our substitute. Jesus is truly the Lamb of God.

4. The unbroken bones

John tells us that the Jewish leaders asked Pilate to have his soldiers break the legs of Jesus and the two men crucified either side of him. They asked this because the Sabbath was drawing near. Pilate agreed. However, when the soldiers arrived they found Jesus dead so they did not break his legs (19:33). Why is it so important that Jesus' bones were not broken? In Exodus 12:46, the Lord says to Moses, 'Do not break any of the [lamb's] bones.' Again, see how the story of the Passover is finding its fulfilment in the death of Jesus. On the cross, Jesus leads us in an exodus from sin into the promised land of the Father's love, presence and forgiveness. What a glorious freedom!

It is right to begin our study by praying that the day will soon come when both Jews and Gentiles will find unity at the cross of Christ. As the Apostle Paul wrote, the Father's purpose has always been to make peace between Jew and Gentile through the cross of the Messiah. Through the blood of Christ both Jews and Gentiles now have access to the Father in the power of the Holy Spirit (Ephesians 2:11–18). As we have seen throughout this first chapter, the Spirit leads to the cross. So come, Holy Spirit, and lift the veil from darkened minds and hard hearts, both Jew and Gentile (2 Corinthians 3:12–18).

Chapter 2

ANOINTING AND AFFLICTION

*How much more, then, will the blood of Christ, who through
the eternal Spirit offered himself unblemished to God,
cleanse our consciences from acts that lead to death, so that
we may serve the living God!*

Hebrews 9:14

He is the lonely greatness of the world –
  (His eyes are dim).
His power it is holds up the Cross
  That holds up Him.

He takes the sorrow of the threefold hour –
  (His eyelids close).
Round him and round, the wind – His Spirit – where
  It listeth blows.

And so the wounded greatness of the world
  In silence lies –
And death is shattered by the light from out
  Those darkened eyes.

Madeleine Caron Rock[1]

The Roman historian Tacitus wrote of Jesus Christ that 'he suffered *the extreme penalty* during the reign of Tiberius at the hands of the procurator Pontius Pilate' (my italics).[2]

As we come to consider the crucifixion of Jesus, we need to remind ourselves that we are talking about an actual event in history, a fact in space and time. Even the Roman historian Tacitus testifies to the historicity of the Calvary event. Other non-Christian historians of the period do also.

We also need to understand the horror of what Tacitus describes as 'the extreme penalty'. The Gospel records are extremely brief in their descriptions of what happened to Jesus at Golgotha. Mark writes: 'They brought Jesus to the place called Golgotha (which means The Place of the Skull). Then they offered him wine mixed with myrrh, but he did not take it. And they crucified him' (Mark 15:22–24).

Matthew writes: 'They came to a place called Golgotha (which means The Place of the Skull). There they offered Jesus wine to drink, mixed with gall; but after tasting it, he refused to drink it. When they had crucified him, they divided up his clothes by casting lots' (Matthew 27:33–35).

Luke writes: 'When they came to the place called the Skull, there they crucified him, along with the criminals – one on his right, the other on his left' (Luke 23:33).

John writes: 'Carrying his own cross, he went out to the place of the Skull (which in Aramaic is called Golgotha). Here they crucified him, and with him two others – one on each side and Jesus in the middle' (John 19:17–18).

As far as the actual process of crucifixion is concerned, none of the Gospel writers dwells on it at all. Mark says, 'And they crucified him.' Matthew, 'When they had crucified him.' Luke, 'there they crucified him.' John, 'Here they crucified him.' Each of the Gospel writers sums up the final execution of Jesus in one simple Greek verb, *stauro*.

Yet this one word would have produced an immediate

shudder of horror in the ancient world. Today the word 'crucifixion' does not conjure up the obscene and terrifying connotations it once did. But in the time of Jesus (and indeed during the centuries before), everyone who came in contact with the Roman Empire would have seen people crucified, and in Judea crosses were a common enough spectacle. Though the form of crucifixion could vary, the norm consisted of beating the victim, then either tying or nailing him to a plank of wood, hoisting up on a post, to be propped up on a small wooden seat. By the first century after Christ, the Romans had perfected this form of execution. They knew exactly how to prolong survival and increase pain through severing nerves rather than arteries. It was truly a sadistic and barbaric method and was usually reserved for the lower classes and particularly for criminals, slaves, rebels and murderers. Roman citizens were never crucified unless they had deserted as soldiers. Crucifixion was reserved for the lowest of the low.

This was the way in which the high king of heaven died. The one without sin died like a criminal. The master of all died like a slave. The obedient Son died the death of a rebel. The giver of life died like a murderer. This is the great paradox of the cross. As the church father Melito wrote: 'He who hung the earth in its place hangs there, he who fixed the heavens is fixed there, he who made all things fast is made fast upon the tree. The Master has been insulted, God has been murdered, the king of Israel has been killed. . . .'[3] The death that Jesus suffered for our sins was indeed the 'extreme penalty'.

The passion of Jesus

The last twenty-fours of Jesus' life involved so much suffering in such a short space of time that it is impossible to imagine how anyone could have endured it all.

Consider the evidence of the New Testament.[4] Between 6pm on a Thursday evening and the start of the Sabbath twenty-four hours later, Jesus of Nazareth had to go through the following: the deep anxiety of Gethsemane, the arrest, the betrayal, desertion by his friends, Jewish and Roman trials, a severe flogging, the exertion of carrying a heavy plank of wood, the agony of having his wrists nailed to this cross bar, his feet nailed to the upright post after he was hoisted up, a loss of normal respiration, the setting in of shock, exhaustion, asphyxia and death.

If we start with Gethsemane, we read how Jesus suffered intense mental anguish in this quiet olive grove as he contemplated his own death. Jesus experienced a very rare phenomenon that only occurs when a person is in an extremely heightened emotional state. This phenomenon – known as hematidrosis – produces 'bloody sweat'.

There then followed the arrest after Judas betrayed the location of this rendezvous and, in the darkness, identified Jesus to the Temple authorities. Soon after midnight Jesus was taken for an informal, nocturnal interrogation by Annas, followed by a hearing before Caiaphas between about 1am and daybreak. Having been accused of blasphemy, Jesus was then beaten by Caiaphas' guards. After daybreak, Jesus was tried before the Sanhedrin in the Temple and taken before Pilate (since permission for an execution had to be granted by the procurator).

Pilate handed the matter over to Herod Antipas, the tetrarch of Judea, but he, having questioned Jesus, returned him to Pilate, having found no basis for a charge against him. Pilate tried to release Jesus, but the insistent manipulation of the Jewish leaders in Jerusalem forced his hand and he finally, reluctantly agreed to their demands and sentenced Jesus to death.

At this point Jesus would have been exhausted. He had been under arrest for twelve hours already. He had experienced the intense apprehension that had caused blood to be released into his sweat glands. He had been abandoned by his friends and humiliated by his enemies. He had already suffered one beating after his first Jewish trial. He had gone a whole night without any sleep and he had been forced to walk nearly three miles.

There then followed another beating, this time ordered by Pontius Pilate. A scourging was the customary, legal preliminary to every Roman execution. Jesus would have stood for this in the Praetorium. His hands would have been tied to the top of an upright post. He would have been stripped of his clothing. A short whip called the *flagellum* was most frequently used to administer the punishment. This was made up of braided leather thongs of different lengths in which sheep bones or small iron balls were tied at intervals up and down each strip. Two soldiers would have conducted the beating, one each side, giving alternate lashes of their whip on the back and buttocks. As these soldiers repeatedly struck Jesus with their whips, the sharp objects on the leather thongs would have caused deep contusions as they cut into the skin. They would have lacerated the underlying muscles as well. The pain would have been immense and the blood loss considerable.

Then came the soldiers' mockery, in which a robe was placed on Jesus' shoulders, a crown of thorns on his head, and a wooden sceptre in his hand. These soldiers then forced Jesus to carry the *patibulum* or cross bar from the flogging post in the Praetorium (a distance of one third of a mile, though the Cyrenian carried it part of the way). This piece of wood weighed about 100 lbs and was tied to his outstretched arms. Outside the city walls, Jesus was thrown to the ground on his back and nailed to the cross beam. The nails, about six inches long, would have been driven through the median nerve in the centre of each wrist, carefully avoiding the major arteries either side, thereby avoiding a quick death through blood loss, and producing massive bolts of pain through the arms and body.

Jesus was then lifted onto the upright post, called the *stipes*. Four soldiers would have been required for this task. Jesus' feet were nailed to the front of the lower part of the *stipes*, again carefully avoiding arteries, and severing major nerves. Normal respiration would now have been impossible. The weight of the body bearing down on his chest would have fixed intercostal muscles in an inhalation state. Breathing would have become shallow. Muscle cramps would have set in. No bodily movement would have been able to ease the pain, especially since any attempt to do so would result in the wounds on the back scraping against the upright post. The inevitable result would eventually be death by exhaustion, shock, dehydration or asphyxia.

Jesus died relatively quickly – after hanging on the cross for six hours – at approximately 3pm on the Friday afternoon. This was no doubt due to the fact that he had received two beatings, resulting in severe loss of blood (an assertion supported by the fact that Jesus could not carry his own *patibulum* very far). The soldiers had to resort to the practice of *crucifragium* (leg-breaking) in order to hasten the death of the two criminals on either side of Jesus. They found Jesus already dead, but one of the soldiers thrust his infantry spear into Jesus' side in order to make sure, and this resulted in an effusion of pleural fluid as well as blood. It is even possible in the light of this that Jesus died of cardiac rupture (ie, a broken heart).

A dangerous heresy

I have provided this rather detailed description not out of a morbid fascination but because I want to ask the fundamental question, How did Jesus endure such appalling, prolonged agony?

This is particularly relevant for our discussion of the work of the Spirit and the work of the cross. In the first chapter we saw how the Holy Spirit prepared for the Calvary event through the Old Testament prophets. Our focus was on the ministry of the Spirit *before* the cross of Christ. In this chapter I want to look at the work of the Spirit *during* the passion and death of Jesus. In other words, I want to answer the question, Did Jesus receive any divine help at Calvary? Or did he struggle through entirely on his own and with the very limited resources of his own humanity?

The reason such an investigation is needed is that there is, I suspect, a Gnostic tendency in some Christians when it comes to the cross. Gnosticism (sometimes known as Docetism) was a deviant form of Christianity which flowered in the second century after Christ, though the apostles (particularly Paul and John) had to contend with proto-Gnostic factions in the first century. Paul's battle with this kind of thinking is evident in 1 and 2 Corinthians, John's in his gospel and letters.

The Gnostics embraced an extreme form of the Greek dualism between the physical and the spiritual. Putting it simply, the Gnostics believed that the physical and the material were evil, while the spiritual and the mystical were good. The implications for the human body were profound. Since the body is physical, it was seen as evil and contemptible. This either led to asceticism (constantly disciplining the body and its desires) or hedonism (giving free rein to the body and its desires). Either way, the higher life of the heavenly world of *gnosis* (the Greek word for knowledge) was what really mattered.

As Western Christians, we are influenced by the Greek world-view which embraced a dualism of the physical and the spiritual. This impacts many things, including our understanding of Jesus' relationship with the Holy Spirit. The Gnostics taught that the Spirit was not active in Jesus' life prior to his baptism and that the anointing of the Spirit left Jesus before his passion. They simply could not see how the Spirit could have been present and active in either a growing child or a tortured body. For the Gnostics, a physical vessel like this was far too imperfect to accommodate the Spirit.

Yet the Scriptures reveal that the Holy Spirit was at work in Jesus' life well before Jesus' baptism, in fact as early as his conception. In Luke 1:35, the angel Gabriel promises Mary that the Holy Spirit will come upon her and that the power of the Holy Spirit will overshadow her. Here the word 'overshadow' is taken from the language of the hovering presence of the glory cloud in the Old Testament. The very conception of Jesus of Nazareth is therefore a creative miracle of the Holy Spirit. Matthew stresses that Mary was 'with child through the Holy Spirit' (Matthew 1:18). The angel of the Lord further tells Joseph that 'what is conceived in her is from the Holy Spirit' (Matthew 1:20). Though virtually nothing is said about Jesus' relationship with the Spirit from his birth to his baptism, we are surely right to infer that the Spirit was at work in the 'hidden years' while Jesus was growing to full maturity. If John the Baptist could be filled with the Holy Spirit even from the womb (Luke 1:15), are we not right in inferring that, at the very least, the Spirit was active in Jesus' life prior to his baptism?

The Gnostic view that Jesus of Nazareth was not endowed with the Holy Spirit prior to his baptism cannot therefore be sustained. In the one episode recorded about his
boyhood, Luke tells us that Jesus went into the Temple and
that 'everyone who heard him was amazed at his understanding and his answers' (Luke 2:47). Are we not right in
seeing here an early sign of the Spirit's work in Jesus' life –
a sign perhaps of the spiritual gift known as 'the word of
wisdom'? Is there not some case to be made for this being a
mark of Jesus' charismatic authority? It is interesting to my
mind that the source of the amazement in Luke 2:47 is the
level of understanding Jesus possesses. This is significant
because Isaiah prophesied that the Spirit would rest upon
the Messiah, and that this would confer 'the Spirit of wisdom and of understanding' (Isaiah 11:2). For further con-
firmation we should note the fact that the boy Jesus 'grew
in wisdom' (Luke 2:52). The Spirit is therefore at work in
Jesus' life not only prior to his baptism but prior to his *bar
mitzvah* (he was only twelve years old!). It is also worth
noting that the boy Jesus understood the Temple to be his
Father's house. This implies an intimate knowledge of God
as Father and a sense of sonship, both of which are results
of the Spirit's work. In the light of all this, I agree totally
with Gerald Hawthorne:

The Holy Spirit was continuously with him in his silence and
in his speech, in his haste and in his leisure, in company and in
solitude, in his play and in his work, in the freshness of the
morning and the weariness of the evening – throughout all the
hours and days of those early years of his life.[5]

At the Jordan River

If the Holy Spirit was at work from Jesus' conception to his adult life, then why did he need to receive the Holy Spirit in the River Jordan? If he already had the Spirit, why did he need a further endowment at his baptism?

This is an important question. The Gnostics – like many New Agers today – argued that the 'Christ Spirit' came upon Jesus at his baptism but not before. In other words, he was not the Messiah prior to his baptism because the Spirit came upon him for the first time in the Jordan.

However, we need to understand that Jesus already knew he was the Son of God well before this. As we have already seen, as a twelve-year-old boy he had spoken of the Temple as his Father's house. When the Holy Spirit came upon Jesus in the Jordan, this was therefore not the start of a filial relationship between Jesus and God the Father but an affirmation of it. In other words, Jesus' relationship with the Father was already a potent part of his consciousness prior to the baptism. The Holy Spirit, who is the cord of love between the Father and the Son and between the Son and the Father, was already at work in the humanity of Jesus in the hidden years.

Furthermore, Jesus only begins to announce the arrival of the kingdom, and to perform miracles, after his baptism. So the anointing of the Spirit in the River Jordan has to be understood as an empowerment for preaching about and demonstrating the dynamic reign of God on the earth. It is from this moment on that Jesus is anointed with power and set apart for his messianic mission.

The baptism of Jesus is therefore the beginning of something. The descent of the Spirit in the form of a dove implies as much. This recalls the brooding of the Spirit like a bird at the beginning of Creation (Genesis 1:2). Jesus' baptism does not mark the beginning of his relationship with the Father, but the beginning of his kingdom mission (God's new creative work) is here. As the Apostle Peter was later to say:

> You know what has happened throughout Judea, beginning in Galilee after the baptism that John preached – how God anointed Jesus of Nazareth with the Holy Spirit and power, and how he went around doing good and healing all who were under the power of the devil, because God was with him.
>
> Acts 10:37–38

At his baptism, Jesus was filled with the Holy Spirit as never before. But this does not mean that the Spirit was not present in his life prior to that. Indeed, we have already seen that the Spirit was active in him as he was growing up. What Jesus did not have was the anointing to begin preaching about the kingdom in words, and demonstrating the arrival of the kingdom in acts of power. For this reason, Jesus returns from the Jordan and the desert to declare,

> The Spirit of the Lord is on me, because he has anointed me to preach good news to the poor. He has sent me to proclaim freedom for the prisoners and recovery of sight for the blind, to release the oppressed, to proclaim the year of the Lord's favour.
>
> Luke 4:18–19

From this moment on, Jesus was conscious of a new dimension of charismatic power and authority, enabling him to forgive sinners, heal the sick, deliver the oppressed and even raise the dead. With the descent of the dove, a new age had truly dawned. The effects of the Fall could now be reversed. Paradise, one day, could be regained.

Clothed with power

So far we have seen how the Holy Spirit worked in Jesus throughout his earthly life. We have seen how the Spirit created Jesus' body in Mary's womb, how he imparted increasing levels of wisdom and understanding during his childhood and youth, how he possessed a revelation of his unique Sonship, how he was anointed with the power of the Holy Spirit at his baptism, thereby inaugurating the arrival of God's reign.

From then on, Jesus is conscious of divine power at work in his life. Everything he says and does flows out of the plenitude of the Spirit's anointing. He is sent out by the Spirit into the wilderness to war against Satan. He returns full of the Holy Spirit to announce that Isaiah 61 is now going to be fulfilled in his ministry. With the Spirit of the sovereign Lord upon him, Jesus now preaches that the kingdom is near and begins his ministry of healing and deliverance. Matthew writes that this ministry is proof that Jesus of Nazareth is the Spirit-anointed Messiah of Isaiah 42:1–4 (Matthew 12:15–21). As if to underline the point, Matthew a few verses later reports Jesus' telling his listeners that it is by the Spirit of God that he casts out demons (Matthew 12:28). It is through the power of the Spirit that Jesus destroys the works of the evil one.

Jesus not only performs actions that are clearly inspired by the Spirit, he also speaks words that are evidently the result of charismatic revelation. His teaching ministry is endowed with divine authority. Whereas the prophets spoke the word of the Lord ('thus says the Lord'), Jesus speaks in the first person, 'Truly, truly I say to you.' Not only that, Jesus also speaks with prophetic insight. He knows by charismatic revelation the condition of a person's heart. This knowledge is not gained by human learning but through knowledge mediated by the Holy Spirit. John writes in his Gospel,

> Now while he was in Jerusalem at the Passover Feast, many people saw the miraculous signs he was doing and believed in his name. But Jesus would not entrust himself to them, for he knew all men. He did not need man's testimony about man, for he knew what was in a man.
>
> John 2:23–25

Thus Jesus' speech is just as inspired as his actions. In fact it is through charismatic words and works that the kingdom is manifested in his ministry. The message and the miracles are woven together to form a tapestry portraying the reign of God on the earth.

From his baptism onwards, Jesus is therefore aided and empowered by the Holy Spirit in everything. But what of the final twenty-four hours of his life? What of Gethsemane? The arrest? The trials? The floggings? The Calvary road? The cross itself? Where was the Holy Spirit during these hours of agony? Did the Spirit leave Jesus before he took up his cross, as the Gnostics once taught, and as their modern counterparts (the New Agers) contend?

An anointing for affliction

It is important at this point to return to the baptism of Jesus. Mark's Gospel has an interesting detail which is often missed. While Matthew and Luke say that the heavens are opened, Mark reports that they are torn open (Mark 1:10). The verb translated 'torn' is only used one other time in the Gospel, in Mark 15:38, when Mark says that the veil of the Temple was torn in two from top to bottom. In doing this, Mark has employed what is technically known as an 'inclusio'. This is a rhetorical device commonly used in the ancient world whereby an author ends a passage or a book with echoes of their beginning. How does Mark use this literary technique? At the beginning of his Gospel, we see the heavens torn open and the Father declaring that Jesus is his Son. Towards the end of his Gospel, we see Jesus dying on the cross, the Temple curtain torn from top to bottom, and the centurion on duty declaring that Jesus is God's Son.

These parallels between Jesus' baptism and his death show that for Mark the Jordan experience was an anointing for sacrifice as well as an empowerment for service. This becomes even clearer in Mark 10 when James and John make their bid to sit at Jesus' right and left hand in glory. Jesus asks them, 'Can you . . . be baptised with the baptism I am baptised with?' (Mark 10:38). Here Jesus is obviously referring to his death, likening death on the cross to the death we must die in baptism. This is confirmed at the conclusion of this particular story by Jesus' summary of the purpose of his mission, 'The Son of Man did not come to be served, but to serve, and to give his life as a ransom for many' (Mark 10:45).

When the Holy Spirit descended upon Jesus at his baptism like a dove, Jesus was enabled and empowered not only to perform signs and preach with authority. He was also anointed to give his life as a ransom for many. He was endowed with the power for martyrdom as well as miracles. That being the case, we should see evidence of the work of the Spirit in the period from Jesus' anxiety in Gethsemane until the moment of his death at Calvary.

Passion and power

A brief study of the last hours of the Messiah Jesus proves that the Holy Spirit was with him, giving him the grace to endure his sufferings. In other words, the Spirit's power was present in the Son's passion.

Take Gethsemane. In the garden, Jesus prays, '*Abba*, Father, everything is possible for you' (Mark 14:36). The use of the *Abba* cry in Jesus' prayer is evidence of the work of the Spirit in Jesus' life. The Apostle Paul stresses in two of his letters that this familiar and affectionate way of addressing God in prayer is the result of the Spirit's presence in the heart of a believer (Galatians 4:6; Romans 8:15). The Holy Spirit is the fire of divine love in our hearts, enabling us to enjoy the same relational intimacy with the Father as the Son had in the days of his flesh. The *Abba* cry in Gethsemane shows that the Spirit is far from absent in Jesus' life at this point. Even as he sweats blood, the Son cries out for his Father, and he does so in the power of the Spirit. The Father answers the prayer of the Son by sending an angel to strengthen him (Luke 22:43). It is hard to imagine a more obvious example of charismatic revelation and supernatural assistance than this.

Take next the arrest of Jesus. John reports that Judas guided a detachment of soldiers to Gethsemane and that Jesus stood at the entrance and declared, 'I am he' (meaning, 'I am the one you want'). As he says this, the soldiers fall to the ground, literally floored by Jesus' display of divine authority (John 18:1–6). This should be seen as a manifestation of Spirit-endowed authority. Again, the Holy Spirit is far from absent at the arrest. Jesus even has time to perform one final healing miracle, the restoration of Malchus' ear that Peter so impetuously severs (Luke 22:51).

What of Jesus' interrogations and trials? There are no miraculous acts performed by Jesus during these lonely hours. Now is the time for power to be revealed through weakness, not through wonders. Jesus therefore refrains from demonstrating his heavenly authority. He does not comply with Herod's desire for a miracle (Luke 23:8). He refuses to call upon the angelic armies of heaven even though he is the king of a heavenly kingdom (Matthew 26:53; John 18:36). He will not use his prophetic gift to identify those who are assaulting him while he is blind-folded (Luke 22:64). As Tom Smail puts it, the victory achieved at Calvary is not won 'by a divine superman hurling supernatural laser beams of irresistible energy against a cowering demonic host, but by a lonely suffering man in physical agony, forsaken by his friends and by his Father'.[6]

Where, then, is the evidence of the Spirit's work during the trials of Jesus? The answer is in the words of Jesus uttered during his interrogations. In Mark 13:11, Jesus encourages his disciples that they will be given divine wisdom when they are persecuted in the future: 'Whenever you are arrested and brought to trial, do not worry before-hand about what to say. Just say whatever is given you at the time, for it is not you speaking, but the Holy Spirit.'

Jesus said these words just before his passion and death. If this promise of Spirit-inspired wisdom was to be true for the disciples, how much more was it to be true for the mas-ter? Throughout his interrogations, Jesus appears alone before the ruling authorities of the Roman Empire and the nation of Israel. He says very few words, because he is like a sheep that is silent before her shearers (Isaiah 53:7). Nevertheless, he is not alone. The Spirit stands with the Son, revealing the wisdom of the Father.

What of the events that follow? I am referring to the

floggings, the road to the cross, and the crucifixion itself.
Where is the Holy Spirit in the very last stretch of the race
that Jesus ran? Certainly there are no demonstrations of
the Spirit's power in signs and wonders. Yet, according to
Luke, there is prophecy and there is prayer. Jesus speaks
to the women who mourn and wail for him on the way to
Golgotha, prophesying that a time is coming when they
will be weeping for themselves rather than him (Luke
23:27–31). This is commonly thought to be a prophecy concerning the destruction of Jerusalem forty years later.
There is also Jesus' statement to the penitent thief, 'I tell
you the truth, today you will be with me in paradise'
(Luke 23:43). The use of 'I tell you the truth' (*Amen* in
Greek) shows that this is an example of authoritative
charismatic speech. The future orientation of the words
also suggests that this can be regarded as prophetic utterance: 'Today you *will* be with me.'

Between these two prophecies Luke reports the prayer
of Jesus, 'Father, forgive them, for they do not know what
they are doing' (Luke 23:34). Here the groaning of the
Spirit is vocalised in an extraordinary prayer, uttered in the
place of greatest weakness (Romans 8:26). Using the
imperative, Jesus musters the last ounce of his strength to
command the Father's forgiveness upon his executioners.
Or, as Minka Shura Sprague puts it: 'Spinal column
anchored fast, his limbs secure against the wood, he mar-
shals the last bit of incarnated flesh that he can move. In
breath traversing vocal cord and lung, he prays in the
imperative mood, flings the force of forgiveness across
heaven and earth.'[7]

Here the Spirit intercedes through the crucified Son,
appealing to the Father's heart to have mercy and compassion on the bystanders at the cross, pleading on the
grounds of their ignorance.

From these brief comments, we can therefore legitimately conclude that the work of the Spirit did not stop short of Calvary in Jesus' life. The same Spirit who was intimately involved in the beginning of Jesus' life is intimately involved in the end of Jesus' life, and indeed every moment between. The Gnostic heresy (which, among other things, promoted the view that the Spirit left Jesus before his sufferings began) cannot be sustained on the evidence of the Gospel records. The Holy Spirit enabled and empowered Jesus in Gethsemane, in the palaces of Caiaphas, Herod and Pilate, on the road to Golgotha and on the cross itself. Jesus was given divine power to endure the agony of his passion and death. Though he was lonely at Golgotha, he was not alone.

By the eternal Spirit

A passage in the Epistle to the Hebrews helps us here. Hebrews is a difficult book for a modern Gentile reader. It is full of symbolism taken from the Old Testament world of sacrifice. Its main theme, however, is fairly easy to grasp – the superiority of Jesus to the old covenant way of dealing with sin. In Hebrews, we are given a vision of the priest who offers himself as victim.

In Hebrews 9, the writer deals with the ministry of the high priest on the day of Atonement. In the Tabernacle, the Holy Place was separated from the inner sanctuary (the Holy of Holies) by a curtain. Only the high priest was allowed to enter this most sacred chamber, and once a year at Yom Kippur (the day of Atonement). On that day the high priest would pass through the veil into the inner room, where he would daub the mercy seat with the blood of an animal. This sacrifice was made in order that his sins, and the sins of the people that had been committed in ignorance, might be covered. Rituals like these, however, were an ineffective means of dealing with the sin problem. Every Yom Kippur, the Holy Spirit would be revealing to God's people the inadequacy of this approach and by implication pointing ahead to the superior way that would one day be provided when Jesus died for our sins (Hebrews 9:8ff). On that day the curtain of the Temple would be torn from top to bottom as a signal that the old way of atonement was now obsolete and that the new way, established at Calvary, had begun. As a result of his death, Jesus – our great high priest – would open up the Most Holy Place of the Father's presence through his own precious blood, and he would do this once and for all.

At this point, the writer makes a startling comment concerning the difference between the old and the new way of atonement:

> The blood of goats and bulls and the ashes of a heifer sprinkled on those who are ceremonially unclean sanctify them so that they are outwardly clean. How much more, then, will the blood of Christ, who through the eternal Spirit offered himself unblemished to God, cleanse our consciences from acts that lead to death, so that we may serve the living God!
>
> Hebrews 9:13–14

Here the writer points to the superiority of the new over the old system of atonement. The differences between Calvary (the new) and Yom Kippur (the old) are these: first of all, at Calvary Jesus' sacrifice was voluntary (he offered himself). At Yom Kippur, the sacrifice was involuntary (the animals did not volunteer). Secondly, at Calvary Jesus' sacrifice resulted in internal cleansing. At Yom Kippur, the sacrifice resulted only in external cleansing. Thirdly, at Calvary Jesus offered himself 'through the eternal Spirit'.

At Yom Kippur, the high priest made the offering purely in his own strength.

It is this last thought which is so intriguing, that Jesus offered up his life *dia pneumatos aioniou*, through the eternal Spirit (as the New International Version renders it). The word *dia* means 'through' or 'by'. The word *pneumatos* comes from the noun *pneuma*, meaning 'spirit'. The word *aioniou* comes from the adjective *aionios*, meaning 'everlasting'. On the surface it all looks plain: Jesus gave up his life with the assistance of the everlasting Spirit of God. The Son was helped at Calvary by the Spirit.

But does it really mean this? Some have argued not. They point out that *pneuma* can mean 'the spirit of a man'. They also state that there is no definite article, no reference to it being 'the' Spirit. From this they conclude that the writer is saying that Jesus offered himself unblemished to God not through the Holy Spirit but through his own eternal nature. His sacrifice is eternally effective precisely because it came from one who is everlasting in nature.

However, this is not as strong an argument as it looks. It is true that *pneuma* can be translated 'spirit' (lower case). But there are five good reasons for believing that it has to refer to the Holy Spirit.

First of all, the writer says that Jesus offered himself to God. Is not his own spirit included in the word 'himself'? To say, 'by his own eternal nature he offered himself' is to say virtually the same thing twice.

Secondly, if the writer had wanted us to translate *pneuma* as a reference to the eternal 'nature' of Jesus, there were other Greek words he could have used to make that clear.

Thirdly, the writer has just spoken of the Holy Spirit in verse 8 of this passage, and there he used *pneuma*. It is hard to imagine him thinking of anything other than this 'Holy

Spirit' when, a matter of a few sentences later, he speaks of the 'eternal Spirit'.

Fourthly, the idea of Jesus offering himself by the eternal Spirit makes perfect sense in its context. The writer has just said that the Holy Spirit was at work in the old system of sacrifice. If the Spirit was involved in the old, how much more so in the new!

Fifthly, we need to remember the findings of the last chapter. Isaiah prophesied that the Holy Spirit would anoint the servant of Yahweh for his messianic mission, a mission that would include and culminate in his vicarious suffering (Isaiah 53). The idea that Jesus offered himself at Calvary through the power of the Holy Spirit is well within the orbit of the themes of the servant songs.

What about the matter of the lack of a definite article? The writer does not refer to '*the* eternal Spirit'. There is no article in front of *pneumatos*. Surely this shows that the writer had Jesus' spirit in mind. But this again is not decisive. There are 101 instances in the New Testament where there is no definite article and where the *power* rather than the person of the Holy Spirit is implied. So this cannot be used as an argument against a reference to the *Spirit* in Hebrews 9:14.

The best exposition would therefore seem to be this: 'through the power of the eternal Spirit, Christ offered himself to God as a perfect sacrifice for sins'. Jesus endured his sufferings with the assistance of the Spirit who lives for ever (ie, the third person of the Trinity). The cross of Christ is consequently a trinitarian event. The Son offers himself as the unblemished lamb prophesied by John the Baptist. The offering is made to the Father in heaven, whose justice requires the shedding of blood for effective atonement. The Spirit of God – the eternal bond between the Son and the Father – helps Jesus in his sufferings, thereby making at-one-ment between mortal humans and the God who is from everlasting to everlasting.

The cry of the Son

One pressing question remains. If the Spirit assists and enables Jesus to endure the excruciating agonies of the passion, then why does Jesus cry out, 'My God, my God, why have you forsaken me?' (Mark 15:34). If the Spirit is the bond of love between the Son on earth and the Father in heaven, then surely the Spirit must have departed from Jesus at this point? For Jesus to sense this profound level of abandonment, then at this moment Jesus surely cannot be offering himself to God through the eternal Spirit.

Here we cross the border into mystery. On the one hand we have said that there is evidence of the Spirit's activity in the last hours of Jesus' life. The moments of prophetic utterance and compassionate intercession recorded by Luke seem conclusive on that score. On the other hand it seems as if the Spirit must have left Jesus for him to cry with such utter desolation.

As we grapple with this issue it is vital that we recognise the reality of the sense of rejection in Jesus' mind. Jesus quotes the beginning of Psalm 22 when he declares, 'My God, my God, why have you forsaken me?' Even though this is a quotation, the use of the word 'God' rather than 'Father' is striking. This is the only moment in which Jesus seemingly cannot use the word *Abba* in prayer to God. It seems that there is in Jesus' weakening consciousness a catastrophic rupture of relationship between himself and his Father. As the weight of the world's sin is placed upon his frail shoulders, Jesus senses the Father turning his face away. Now the Son knows what it is to be truly and profoundly alone, feeling God-forsaken in a brutal world.

It seems, then, that the Spirit must have departed from Jesus at the moment when his cry of desolation goes up to heaven. Is this true, however? Could it be that this is not the whole picture? Could it be that the Spirit of the Father is still with the Son even though the Son does not sense that he is still with his Father? Could it be that objectively the Son is not alone, but that subjectively he senses that he is alone?

My own conviction is that even at this moment, when Jesus senses a loss of intimate communion with the Father, the Spirit is still present with him. 'My God, my God why have you forsaken me?' This may not begin with the word '*Abba*' but it is still prayer, and the prayer of Jesus is the cry of the Son to the Father in heaven – a cry urged by the Spirit.

Furthermore, the very quotation itself is evidence of the Spirit's activity. When the Holy Spirit is poured out at Pentecost, Peter will say, 'This is that' (Acts 2:16). 'This is what was spoken by the prophet Joel.' The ability to see present experience as harmonious with past Scripture is regarded as a sign of the work of the Spirit. It constitutes evidence that the Holy Spirit has written God's word on one's heart. Therefore, Jesus' quotation from Psalm 22:1 is itself a sign of the work of the Spirit in his life. He too (as Peter later) is saying, 'This is that.'

Even at Calvary, then, in Jesus' sense of the Father's absence, the Spirit is still present. Even here the Son is still offering himself to the Father through the eternal Spirit. As Calvin once put it, 'Christ suffered as a man, but in order that his death might effect our salvation, it came forth from the power of the Spirit' (*Epistle of Paul to the Hebrews*).

The power to endure

The presence of the Spirit throughout the passion of Jesus should not, of course, imply that his sufferings at Calvary were nothing. Yet, at the same time, we can say that the Holy Spirit gave Jesus the power to endure his sufferings and we can find biblical justification for this in Paul's prayer in Colossians 1:10–11:

> And we pray this in order that you may live a life worthy of the Lord and may please him in every way: bearing fruit in every good work, growing in the knowledge of God, being strengthened with all power according to his glorious might so that you may have great endurance and patience.

In this prayer we see the clearest connection between the endowment of the Spirit and the ability to endure suffering. The word translated 'patience' is *makrothumia*, which Paul identifies as a fruit of the Spirit in Galatians 5:22. Professor Gordon Fee's thoughts at this point are well worth quoting:

> It is perhaps worthy of note that this empowering text has nothing to do with 'signs and wonders' and everything to do with patience and endurance in the present struggle. The power of the Spirit in Paul thus reflects a full-orbed understanding of Christian life, as both already and not yet, which includes both the miraculous, on the one hand, and patient endurance in the midst of hardship on the other. And he simply does not see these two kinds of empowering as being in opposition to one another.[8]

Here we see a vital principle: the same Spirit that empowers us for preaching and healing empowers us for patience and endurance. If we live in this integrated life of the

Spirit, we walk in the footsteps of Jesus. The Spirit of God enabled Jesus both to perform miracles and to endure terrible trials and tribulations. As we have seen through the course of this present chapter, the Spirit led Jesus to the cross and gave him the power of God's might to endure his suffering patiently. This should not offend us as it offended the Gnostics. If the Holy Spirit could lead Jesus to the desert to conquer Satan, why could he not lead Jesus to the cross to triumph there? Yes, there is truly an anointing in affliction.

What could be of greater comfort to believers facing hardship today? The same Spirit who enabled the crucified Messiah to endure what Tacitus described as 'the extreme penalty' is at work in us as well. In times of difficulty, we therefore do not walk alone. When our bodies experience pain, we do not suffer in isolation. When people mock us for confessing the name of Jesus, we do not stand forsaken by God. When loved ones reject or abandon us, the Spirit of God does not cease to be our hidden but present friend. We walk in that same Spirit who inhabited the body of the dying Jesus. It is this revelation that makes victors out of victims.

Chapter 3

PASSOVER AND PENTECOST

But I tell you the truth: It is for your good that I am going away. Unless I go away, the Counsellor will not come to you; but if I go, I will send him to you.

John 16:7

It is from the crucified one in glory that the Spirit comes. The cross was to him the path and the power through which alone he could receive the Spirit to pour out.

Andrew Murray, *The Cross of Christ*.[1]

The cross was not a full stop but a semi-colon; on the third day, Jesus was raised from death by the power of the Holy Spirit. The heavy stone at the entrance of the tomb was miraculously moved. Jesus folded his grave clothes, and then departed. What a sublime victory! As the hymn writer puts it:

Thine be the glory, risen, conquering Son,
Endless is the victory Thou o'er death hast won;
Angels in bright raiment rolled the stone away,
Kept the folded grave-clothes, where Thy body lay.

Recent research has unveiled the significance of the folded grave-clothes.[2] John tells us in his Gospel that the head-cloth ('napkin', KJV) was neatly folded on its own while the strips of linen that had been wound round his body were left lying there (John 20:6–7). Why does John make such a point of the fact that the napkin was left folded?

In the Jewish culture of Jesus' day, there were certain social conventions to observe if you were invited out to a meal. If you enjoyed the meal, you crumpled up your napkin and left it on your place setting. This was your way of saying, 'I've really enjoyed this experience. I'd love to come back.' If, on the other hand, the hospitality had been poor, the service unfriendly, and the food terrible, you folded your napkin and left it very purposefully and neat-ly in front of you. This was your way of saying, 'I have not enjoyed this experience. I don't intend ever to come back!'

Jesus' first act, having been raised from death, was to fold the napkin – the *soudarion* or headcloth – that had formed part of his burial clothes. John writes that it was the sight of this folded garment that evoked faith in the beloved disciple (John 20:8). Why is this apparently redun-dant detail worth mentioning? If we take seriously the con-nection with Jewish meal-table conventions, then the answer is clear. Jesus was saying, 'I have not enjoyed this experience and I don't ever intend going through this again.' In other words, Jesus was telling his disciples (who were Jews, and used to being invited out for meals with their master) that this was no temporary resuscitation, like Lazarus'. This was a permanent resurrection. Lazarus would have to go through the experience of death all over again. Not so Jesus.

The resurrection of Jesus is a victorious miracle performed by the power of his Holy Spirit. It is the Holy Spirit that raised Jesus from death (Romans 8:11). This underlines a great truth: *just as Jesus gave himself up to death through the power of the eternal Spirit, so he conquered death through the power of the eternal Spirit.* The Scriptures may be silent about the work of the Spirit on Holy Saturday, but they are not silent about his work on Easter Sunday. Thus the Apostle Peter writes that Jesus was 'put to death in the body but made alive by the Spirit' (1 Peter 3:18).[3] The Apostle Paul regarded the event of the resurrection as the work of the Spirit (Romans 8:11), and in 1 Timothy 3:16 he says that Jesus 'appeared in a body, was vindicated by the Spirit'. The reference to Jesus being 'vindicated by the Spirit' points to the resurrection. As elsewhere,[4] Paul links the work of the resurrection with the work of the Spirit.

All this shows how important it is to recognise the chain of events which are linked by the Spirit and which find their culmination at Pentecost. First of all, there is the cross. We have already explored the work of the Spirit in relation to Calvary in the previous chapter. Secondly, there is the resurrection, and I have already shown that this too was the result of the work of the Spirit. Thirdly, there was the ascension of Jesus forty days later. This again was a consequence of the dynamic work of the Spirit, as is made clear in Paul's prayer for the church in Ephesus. He prayed that every believer would know the incomparably great power of God the Father expressed through the Holy Spirit in their lives. He then goes on to define the measureless potential of this supernatural strength:

> That power is like the working of his mighty strength, which he exerted in Christ when he raised him from the dead and seated him at his right hand in the heavenly realms, far above all rule and authority, power and dominion, and every title that can be given, not only in the present age but also in the one to come.
>
> Ephesians 1:19–21

Here we have the most unequivocal statement in the New Testament concerning the power that caused Jesus to be lifted up. The whole process of his elevation to heaven – including his crucifixion, resurrection and ascension – was achieved through the mighty strength of the Holy Spirit. Just as Jesus was not alone as he was lifted up on the cross, so he was not alone as he was lifted up in his resurrection and ascension. The Spirit empowered the Son at every turn. Even the session (Christ being seated in glory) is described as the work of the Spirit.

An unbroken chain

So we are presented with a chain of history-making events, extending in a period of just over fifty days from Calvary to Pentecost:

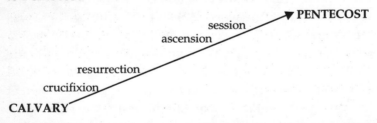

At every point the Spirit empowers the Son in this momentous home-coming to the Father in heaven.

We cannot ignore the fact that Calvary is the divinely

ordained path to Pentecost. If it had not been for the cross, the Spirit could never have been poured out on all flesh. Tom Smail has often recalled the occasion when he spoke in tongues publicly for the first time. After a few moments, a woman in the meeting gave the following interpretation: 'The way to Pentecost is Calvary; the Spirit comes from the cross.'[5] This is exactly the point I want to underline here: God's way to Pentecost was via Calvary. Just as the Spirit leads to the cross, so the cross leads to the Spirit.

This 'unbroken chain' is the theme of the very first sermon after Pentecost. The Apostle Peter explains the manifestation of God's Spirit with reference to Joel 2:28ff. He then starts to preach about Jesus, beginning:

> Men of Israel, listen to this: Jesus of Nazareth was a man accredited by God to you by miracles, wonders and signs, which God did among you through him, as you yourselves know. This man was handed over to you by God's set purpose and foreknowledge; and you, with the help of wicked men, put him to death by nailing him to the cross.
>
> Acts 2:22–23

Peter begins his message with a brief statement of Jesus' ministry. He stresses the work of the Spirit in verse 22. But he majors on the work of the cross in verse 23. In other words, Peter puts Calvary firmly and confrontationally before his listeners, stating that they were responsible for Jesus' crucifixion. The Jesus of Peter's preaching is therefore Christ crucified.

There then follows a long section focusing on the resurrection of Jesus, ending with the magnificent statement, 'God has raised this Jesus to life, and we are all witnesses of the fact' (Acts 2:32). After these verses about the resurrection, Peter moves on to the ascension and the session of

Christ, concluding, 'Let all Israel be assured of this: God has made this Jesus, whom you crucified, both Lord and Christ' (vv.33–36).

As Peter paints a picture of Jesus seated at the right hand of God, he turns to the events of Pentecost, saying, 'He has received from the Father the promised Holy Spirit and has poured out what you now see and hear' (v.33). Notice the subject of the main verb here. It is the exalted Jesus who pours out the Holy Spirit. He is the Lord of the Spirit. Having received the Spirit from his Father, *the Son* opens the floodgates of heaven.

Peter therefore begins his message with Calvary (vv.22–23) and ends it with Pentecost (vv.33–36). Between these two great events, he describes the resurrection, ascension and session of Jesus Christ. For Peter, Calvary is the path to Pentecost. The cross leads to the Spirit.

The feasts of Judaism

Jesus died during the feast of Passover and he poured out the gift of the Holy Spirit at the feast of Pentecost. If we are to understand the rich connection between the death of Christ and the gift of the Spirit, then we have to spend some time looking at these two Jewish feasts. As we do so, we will see that the Father had already established a connection between Passover and Pentecost in the old covenant era, and that this itself was a prophetic preparation for the great fusion of the death of Christ and the outpouring of the Spirit. Indeed, we will see here evidence of God's sovereign planning of events.

Passover and Pentecost were (and are) the two major spring feasts in Judaism. The first, Passover (known as *pesach*), celebrates the exodus or departure of more than a million Israelite slaves from Egypt 3,500 years ago. It is a festival of liberation in which God's people remember how they painted the blood of an unblemished lamb on their doors, how the angel of death passed over them, and how Pharaoh subsequently agreed to Moses' demand, 'Let my people go.' The Passover is celebrated every year as one of the Lord's appointed feasts (Leviticus 23). It is the means by which the memory of Israel's deliverance and redemption is kept alive in every generation. Passover falls in March or April, in the Hebrew month of Nisan.

Between Passover and Pentecost there were two other feasts. The first, the feast of Unleavened Bread, occurs the day after Passover. If Passover falls on 14th Nisan, this feast falls on the 15th and lasts seven days. Its purpose is to remind God's people of the time when they had to leave Egypt in such a hurry that they only had time to cook bread without yeast (Exodus 12:39). During this feast each Jewish family removes the leaven from their homes. Great energy is exerted in trying to identify and destroy every trace of dough in a Jewish building and territory.

The other biblical feast between Passover and Pentecost was the feast of Firstfruits. This was to occur on the second day of the seven-day festival of Unleavened Bread (16th Nisan). At this time the barley was beginning to ripen in Israel, and so the first sheaf of the barley crop was cut and presented to the Lord. In the days of Jesus these firstfruits were brought to the priests in the Temple, who then waved them before the Lord for his acceptance (Deuteronomy 26:1–10; Leviticus 23:11–13).

This sheaf of barley was known as the *omer* (meaning 'measure'). The gathering of the first *omer* on 16th Nisan was important because it marked the countdown to Pentecost. From this day on, the people counted seven weeks of seven days, forty-nine days in all (Leviticus 23:15–16). This period of time was characterised by expectancy, rather like the countdown to Christmas in Western homes today. The practice was known as *Sefirat Ha-Omer*, the Counting of the Omer. Today, the feast of Firstfruits is no longer celebrated because there is no longer a Temple in Jerusalem. It was destroyed in AD 70.

At last, on the fiftieth day after Firstfruits, the second major spring festival occurred, the feast of Weeks (*Hag Hashavuot*, Exodus 34:22). We know this feast by its Greek name, Pentecost (meaning 'fiftieth'). This feast was called *Shavuot* or 'Weeks' because of the seven weeks of preparation that preceded it. It was also known as *Atzeret*, or 'culmination', referring to the fact that the forty-nine days of counting had now concluded.

If Passover celebrated the exodus from Egypt, Pentecost came to be associated with the covenant made at Mount Sinai. This connection was not formally established until AD140, but the link would have been seen well before that, and certainly by the time of Jesus. The giving of the Law at Sinai had originally occurred in the third month (Exodus 19:1). Since the first month of the religious year was the time of Passover, the Rabbis would have concluded well before AD140 that the Sinai event had coincided with the time of *Shavuot*. After the formalisation of this connection in AD140, Pentecost was commonly referred to as *Zeman Mattan Toratenu*, 'The Time of the Giving of our Law'. Pentecost was therefore linked with the giving of the Law, accompanied by fire, at Sinai.

Pentecost was one of three solemn festivals. The other two were Passover and Tabernacles. All three are harvest festivals. In Jesus' day, people were commanded to make pilgrimage to Jerusalem for all three. In the case of Pentecost, the firstfruits of the wheat harvest were brought to the Temple (Leviticus 23:15–21). Two flat loaves of leavened bread made from the wheat were used as a wave offering. For this reason Pentecost was also known as the feast of Harvest.

The completion of Judaism

Jesus of Nazareth came to fulfil and not to abolish Torah. Therefore it should come as no surprise that each of these feasts is fulfilled in the life of Jesus. It is particularly rewarding to see how these feasts came to be completed in the time between the death of Jesus and the outpouring of the Holy Spirit on the day of Pentecost.

If we take Passover first, we have already seen in Chapter 1 how Jesus' death coincided with this feast and how Jesus takes the place of the Passover lambs. Jesus' death occurs on 14th Nisan. Keep in mind that the biblical reckoning of days is different from the modern Western reckoning. For us, a day begins at midnight and ends the following midnight. In Judaism, a day begins at 6pm in the evening and finishes the following evening at the same time. Jesus dies as the sin-bearing lamb of God on the afternoon of 14th Nisan, ie the Friday of Passover at about 3pm. Though the dating of Matthew, Mark and Luke differs from that of John, all four Gospels agree that Jesus is the fulfilment of Passover and that a new covenant is established through his blood.

Jesus' body was buried in a new tomb before the 14th Nisan ended at 6pm. It remained there throughout the Feast of Unleavened Bread on 15th Nisan which was a sacred Sabbath. We might say that Jesus rested on the holy day from his great work of redemption.

This feast involved the removal of leaven, and leaven was a common symbol of sin in the time of Jesus. This is why Paul was later to say to the believers in Corinth:

Your boasting is not good. Don't you know that a little yeast works through the whole batch of dough? Get rid of the old yeast that you may be a new batch without yeast – as you really are. For Christ, our Passover lamb, has been sacrificed. Therefore let us keep the Festival, not with the old yeast, the yeast of malice and wickedness, but with bread without yeast, the bread of sincerity and truth.

1 Corinthians 5:6–8

How might we link all this with the burial of Jesus? Jesus is the bread of life (John 6:35) and bread becomes a symbol of his body in the Lord's Supper. Jesus' dead body saw no corruption in the tomb during 14th, 15th and 16th Nisan. The reason for this, given by Peter in his first message at Pentecost, was because Jesus was the Holy One (ie sinless, Acts 2:27,31). His body was like bread without leaven. Jesus of Nazareth was therefore the fulfilment of the feast of Unleavened Bread.

Then came the feast of Firstfruits. Jesus died on the afternoon of 14th Nisan, day 1. His sinless body rested in the tomb throughout the Sabbath of 15th Nisan, day 2. Then, in the early hours of the morning on 16th Nisan, Jesus was raised from death, day 3. On the third day (according to the Jewish reckoning of time), Jesus rose from the dead. More importantly, on the day of the feast of Firstfruits, the firstfruit of the resurrection was gathered in. The firstfruits of the barley harvest were always the finest, the best, the choicest of the crop. Jesus is the first and the pre-eminent of countless believers who will be resurrected. As Paul says in 1 Corinthians 15:20–23:

But Christ has indeed been raised from the dead, the firstfruits of those who have fallen asleep. For since death came through a man, the resurrection of the dead comes also through a man. For as in Adam all die, so in Christ all will be made alive. But each in his own turn: Christ, the firstfruits; then, when he comes, those who belong to him.

Truly, Jesus is the fulfilment of the feast of Firstfruits.

Fifty days later came Pentecost. During the first forty days of that period, the risen Jesus periodically appeared to the apostles, proving to them that he was indeed alive, and teaching them about the kingdom of God (Acts 1:3). Then, on the fortieth day, Jesus ascended to the heavens, but not before telling his followers to wait for the gift of the Spirit. As they counted the *omer* and prayed, their expectation grew and grew. They kept praying for the fire and asking, 'Could this be the day.' At last, on day 50, Jesus pours out his Spirit:

> When the day of Pentecost came, they were all together in one place. Suddenly a sound like the blowing of a violent wind came from heaven and filled the whole house where they were sitting. They saw what seemed to be tongues of fire that separated and came to rest on each of them. All of them were filled with the Holy Spirit and began to speak in other tongues as the Spirit enabled them.
>
> Acts 2:1–4

As the fire of God's Spirit falls upon the 120 disciples, the feast of Pentecost finds its fulfilment. Keep in mind that Pentecost or Shavuot came to be associated with the giving of the Torah at Mount Sinai. In the time of the exile, Jeremiah prophesied that God would make a new covenant with the people of Israel and Judah. Instead of writing his law on tablets of stone, God would put his law in their minds and write it on their hearts. He would once again be Israel's God. He would teach his people himself, and he would forgive their sins (Jeremiah 31:31–33).

This new covenant was put into effect as a result of the finished work of the cross. Just as the blood of animals solemnised the old covenant, so the blood of Christ solemnises the new. For this new covenant to be personalised, Jesus Christ had to live a life of total obedience to death, even death on the cross. He had to do what Israel had failed to do, and keep the covenant perfectly. Furthermore, the fire of God's Spirit was needed as well as the blood of Christ. So Ezekiel prophesied: 'I will give you a new heart and put a new spirit in you; I will remove from you your heart of stone and give you a heart of flesh. And I will put my Spirit in you and move you to follow my decrees and be careful to keep my laws' (Ezekiel 36:26–27).

Jesus of Nazareth – Israel's representative – fulfils the feasts of Pentecost and Passover. Ascended on high, he sends the power of the Spirit to write the message of the cross (the new covenant) on our hearts. As he does so, his work of salvation comes to the point of victorious completion.

The cross leads to the Spirit

All this points to the inseparable connection between Passover and Pentecost in the feasts of Judaism. In the time of Jesus, Passover was a celebration of the Exodus and Pentecost was a celebration of the Sinai event. Passover itself had incorporated the feast of Unleavened Bread as well as the feast of Firstfruits, and had become a single eight-day festival. So the connection looked like this:

DAY 1 (from Firstfruits)   **DAY 50**

Passover ══════════════════════════════➤ **Pentecost**

These two festivals cannot therefore be isolated from one

another. They were linked because they described two stages of the same journey – the exit from Egyptian domination and the entrance into a new stage in the covenant relationship with *Yahweh* (as his holy people). They were also linked by the counting of the *omer* between the day of the feast of Firstfruits and the day of Pentecost. In Judaism, Passover therefore leads to Pentecost.

In the same way, there is an inseparability about the events in which these two festivals find their fulfilment. The death of Christ (Passover) and the giving of the Spirit (Pentecost) must be held together. Between these two pivotal moments lie the events of the resurrection, the ascension and the session of Christ. These build up towards the climactic moment (the *Atseret*, or culmination, we might say) when the ascended Lord pours out the Holy Spirit.

What we have here is the most extraordinary chain of grace. If Christ had not died on the cross, he would not have been raised from death. If he had not been raised from death he would not have ascended to heaven. If he had not ascended he would not have been seated at the right hand of the majesty on high. If he had not taken his place at the Father's right hand, he would not have poured out the Holy Spirit that the Father gave him (Acts 2:33). The cross therefore leads to the Spirit. Calvary, with its victory over sin, was the Son's path to the Spirit.

When John reports that water flowed from the dead body of Jesus on the cross, he is saying that the cross leads to the Spirit (John 19:34–35). John has something of a fascination with water throughout his Gospel, mostly because water is a metaphor for the Holy Spirit. In John 4, Jesus offers the gift of spiritual water to the woman at the well, and this is clearly an image of the Spirit of life. In John 7, Jesus addresses the pilgrims in the Temple at the feast of Tabernacles (where prayer for the rain of the Spirit was at its highest). As the priests are pouring water on the altar of sacrifice in the Temple, Jesus tells them that the thirsty should come to him and drink because streams of living water are available for the believer. John then adds, 'By this he meant the Spirit, whom those who believed in him were later to receive. Up to that time the Spirit had not been given, since Jesus had not yet been glorified' (John 7:39).

In other words, the streams of living water would begin to flow once Jesus was lifted up (through crucifixion, resurrection and ascension) to glory.

John marvels at the water that flows from Jesus' dead body because he regards it as a sign. We cannot go so far as to say that the Holy Spirit is actually poured out in fullness upon the people standing at the foot of the cross. That would do away with the need for Pentecost. What we can say is that John is stating symbolically that the Spirit comes from the cross. Calvary marks the event that makes Pentecost possible.

This is why John quotes from the prophet Zechariah directly after the effusion of water and blood (John 19:37). Zechariah had prophesied a time when the people of Jerusalem would look upon the one they had pierced (the work of the cross, Zechariah 12:10). At the same time, 'a fountain [would] be opened to the house of David and the inhabitants of Jerusalem' (the work of the Spirit, Zechariah 13:1).

This is what John sees happening at Calvary. For him, Jesus' death is part of his lifting up, his glorification, his return to the Father. For him, the crucifixion, resurrection and ascension of Jesus are all part of one upward movement in which the Son goes home to glory. Even at Calvary, therefore, there can be cracks in the dam. Even at the cross, the water can begin to flow because this marks the moment when Jesus started his upward movement to heaven and 'gave up his spirit' (or 'Spirit', John 19:30).

So John is stating in narrative form what the greatest hymn of the Welsh Revival would one day celebrate poetically. During the Revival of 1904-1905 in South Wales, the cross was the theme of many of the new hymns and songs that were inspired by the Spirit. The most popular included these words:

> On the Mount of Crucifixion
> Fountains opened deep and wide;
> Through the floodgates of God's mercy
> Flowed a vast and gracious tide.
> Grace and love, like mighty rivers,
> Poured incessant from above,
> And heaven's peace and perfect justice
> Kissed a guilty world in love.[6]

To your advantage

At this point we begin to see why Jesus' departure at Calvary was good news for the disciples. At the time, of course, it seemed far from that. On the night before Jesus died, the disciples were both confused and upset by the prospect of their master's death. Yet Jesus was adamant that he had to go if the Spirit was to come. So, in the farewell discourses of John 14–16, we come across this statement by Jesus:

> But I tell you the truth: It is for your good that I am going away. Unless I go away, the Counsellor will not come to you; but if I go, I will send him to you. When he comes, he will convict the world of guilt in regard to sin and righteousness and judgment: in regard to sin, because men do not believe in me; in regard to righteousness, because I am going to the Father,

where you can see me no longer; and in regard to judgment, because the prince of this world now stands condemned.

(John 16:7–11)

Here Jesus tells his followers that he is about to leave, adding in verse 7: 'It is for your good.' The King James Version says: 'It is expedient for you.' The Revised Standard Version says: 'It is to your advantage.' The Living Bible says: 'It is best for you.' The Message version says: 'It is better for you.' All these versions are trying to render the Greek verb *sumphero*. This same verb is used by John in 11:50 when Caiaphas says: 'It is better [KJV, expedient] for you that one man [Jesus] die for the people than that the whole nation perish.' In John 16:7, Jesus is saying that his death on the cross is good for the disciples because it is the necessary path to Pentecost. The New Living Translation renders the statement thus: 'But it is actually best for you that I go away, because if I don't the Counsellor won't come. If I do go away, he will come because I will send him to you.'

The Counsellor is of course the Holy Spirit. Jesus has already told the disciples that the Father will give them another Counsellor, the Spirit of truth, who will be with them for ever (John 14:16). He has told them that the Holy Spirit will teach them all things and will remind them of everything that he has said to them (John 14:26). The Spirit will testify about Jesus (John 15:26). Now Jesus tells them that his departure is the means by which the Spirit will come. Thereafter he teaches that the Spirit 'will convict the world of guilt in regard to sin and righteousness and judgment' (John 16:8), and will guide the disciples into all truth (John 16:13). Jesus adds that the Spirit will not speak his own words; he will speak the words that he hears from Jesus, some of which will concern what is yet to come. The

Spirit will bring revelation to the disciples and will bring glory to Jesus (John 16:13–15).

The key thing at this point is to recognise the crucial difference Calvary makes to the relationship between the Holy Spirit and the people of God. We know that the Holy Spirit was active in the old covenant era because we have already seen in this book how he was at work in the lives of the prophets and indeed in the Temple sacrifices. One of the reasons why Jesus' death and departure are such good news is because it will mean that the Holy Spirit will be available to the people of God in a wholly new way. The work of the cross will represent the most profound turning point in history as far as the work of the Holy Spirit is concerned.

There are four new things, in particular, which we should note about the ministry of the Spirit after the cross:

First of all, *the Spirit is now universal not local.* During the ministry of Jesus, the empowering presence of the Holy Spirit was localised in the life of the Son. John says that the Holy Spirit descended like a dove and remained on the Messiah at his baptism (John 1:32). During Jesus' ministry, the Holy Spirit operated in and through the historical Jesus. Where Jesus was, the Spirit was too. After Calvary and Pentecost, the picture is very different. Now, from the right hand of God, the exalted Messiah can pour out the Holy Spirit on everyone who calls upon his name. Jesus says that when the Spirit comes he will convict 'the world'. When this promise is fulfilled on the day of Pentecost, Peter quotes Joel the prophet, 'I will pour out my Spirit on all people' (Acts 2:17). Thanks to Calvary, the Spirit can now be universal not just local.

Secondly, *the Holy Spirit is now general not partial.* In the Old Testament, those who received the Holy Spirit were, for the most part, the prophets, judges, priests and kings.

In Israel, it was only a select few, a charismatic elite, who were anointed by the Holy Spirit. Now, after the death of Jesus, all this changes. No favouritism will be shown with regard to charismatic endowment. The Holy Spirit will not be sexist; he will come upon men and women alike. He will not be ageist; he will come upon old and young alike. He will not be classist; he will come upon servants as well as masters. He will not be racist; he will come upon Gentiles as well as Jews. Thanks to Calvary, the Holy Spirit is now general not partial. Indeed, Pentecost inaugurates a true democracy of the Spirit.

Thirdly, *the Holy Spirit is now internal not external.* In the Old Testament, the Holy Spirit is most commonly portrayed in terms of 'coming upon', or 'clothing' people. The sense is nearly always of select people receiving an external anointing or empowering. This is also true of the disciples prior to the cross. Up until Calvary, Jesus says that the Holy Spirit has only been *with them* (John 14:17). However, after Jesus' departure, the Spirit will no longer be just *'with'* the disciples. He will be *'in'* the disciples. That is why Jesus says, 'You know [the Counsellor], for he lives *with* you and will be *in* you' (John 14:17, my italics). After Jesus' death, the Spirit will no longer be merely an external anointing; he will be an internal reality. Thanks to Calvary, the Spirit will be in the disciples, guiding them into all truth, reminding them of the words of Jesus, testifying about Jesus, and disclosing the things that are to come.

Fourthly, *the Holy Spirit is now permanent not transient.* In the Old Testament, the charismatic anointing of God upon the prophets, judges, priests and kings was not a lasting one. It was a temporary empowering which seems to have lasted for the duration of the task or ministry concerned. Not so after Calvary. Jesus makes the wonderful promise to his disciples that the Counsellor will be with them for ever. In John 14:16 he says, 'I will ask the Father, and he will give you another Counsellor to be with you *for ever* – the Spirit of truth.' Thanks to Calvary, the gift of the Spirit is to be a permanent not a fading phenomenon. The messianic age of the Spirit has now arrived. The last days have begun. The power of the age to come is with us for ever.

Clearly, then, Calvary is extremely expedient for us, at least as far as our relationship with the Holy Spirit is concerned. After the cross, the Spirit will be universal, not local. He will be general, not partial. He will be internal, not external, and he will be permanent, not transient. If Jesus had avoided the way of the cross, if he had not finished the work which the Father had given him (John 5:36), then Pentecost would never have happened, and we would still be in a situation where the gift of the Spirit was local, partial, external and transient. Praise God that this is not the case. Thanks be to God for the uncompromising obedience of Jesus. He went to Calvary, and for the joy set before him endured the shame and agony of the cross. As a result, the Father vindicated his Son by raising him from death and exalting him to the very heights of his throne. From there, the crucified Messiah has poured out the gift of the Spirit on all those who repent of their sins and believe in his name.

The price of Pentecost

In the light of all that we have seen, we need to remind ourselves not to cheapen the price of Pentecost. The ascended Jesus received the promised gift of the Spirit from his Father and then poured out the fire of divine love upon the 120 disciples (Acts 2:33). But the path to this receiving and giving of the Spirit was, for Jesus, a costly one. It was a path of total obedience to death, even death on a cross (Philippians 2:8). From his birth to his death, Jesus chose the Father's way rather than his own way. In the desert, Satan tried to tempt Jesus to receive the kingdoms of the world (which were to be his any way) without going through the ordeal of Calvary. At Gethsemane, Jesus was tempted at the eleventh hour not to go through with the agony of the cross. But he said 'Yes' to his Father and, because of that, the Father highly exalted him and gave him the responsibility of pouring out the Spirit. For Jesus, the cross was the only way to the outpouring of the Spirit. We cannot and must not cheapen the price of Pentecost.

Summary

In Part One of this book we have looked at the *fact* of the cross. In other words, we have looked at the cross as an *event* and examined its relationship with the person and work of the Spirit. In chapter 1 we saw how the Spirit inspired the Old Testament prophets with dreams, visions and messages about the future Calvary event. Here we saw the Spirit preparing for the cross. In chapter 2 we saw how the Spirit led Jesus to the cross. Jesus went to Calvary endued with the Spirit's work. Christ offers himself to the Father through the eternal Spirit (Hebrews 9:14). If the Spirit leads to the cross, so the cross leads to the Spirit. That is the theme of this present chapter.

In Part Two we move from the fact of the cross to the fellowship of the cross. In other words, we move from the life of Jesus to the life of the believer. We need to do this because there is a pressing need for a reconciliation between the cross and the Spirit in our own lives too. As Jesus said, 'No servant is greater than his master' (John 13:16). Too many Christians today are either Calvary Christians or Pentecost Christians. In other words, some emphasise the cross. Others emphasise the Spirit. Some wear crucifixes. Others wear doves. The Calvary Christian focuses on the cross and on the cost of discipleship. The Pentecost Christian focuses on the Spirit and the charismatic life. The truth is that Calvary Christians need to rediscover the kingdom, the power and the glory of the Spirit-filled life. Pentecost Christians need to recapture a vision of taking up one's own cross daily in a life of spiritual discipline and dedicated service.

If we want revival in our community, our nation, then we cannot bypass the cross and we cannot stand aloof to the empowering presence of God's Spirit. Revivals are seasons ordained by God in which the Holy Spirit becomes present in a manifest way in a community, leading to salvation, healing and deliverance on an impressive scale. The path to such seasons is, however, costly. Church history is full of people who were called to total consecration and surrender as they desperately prayed for such a day of power. They had to press in with selfless perseverance before they saw the kingdom advance in power.

In the Old Testament, the fire falls at the time of sacrifice. In the New Testament, the Spirit comes down after the Son has been lifted up. We therefore need to heed the warning of Andrew Murray:

> Let all who pray for revival and the outpouring of the Spirit pray for a revival of the religion of the cross, with all it meant to our Lord; the revival of the Spirit's mighty working will follow soon. It is God's unalterable law in delivering us from sin and the world: the cross leads to the Spirit.[7]

Part Two

The Life of the Believer

Chapter 4

FULLNESS AND FAITH

When he [the Spirit] comes, he will convict the world of guilt in regard to sin and righteousness and judgment.

John 16:8

If the spirit that is at work among a people is plainly observed to work so as to convince them of Christ. . . . and that he is the Son of God, and was sent by God to save sinners . . . it is a sure sign that it is the true and right Spirit.

Jonathan Edwards, *The Distinguishing Marks of a Work of the Spirit of God.*[1]

Saving Private Ryan is probably the most realistic, vivid and powerful war film ever made. Directed by Stephen Spielberg and starring Tom Hanks, the film tells the story of a team of American soldiers led by Captain John Miller (played by Hanks). After landing at Normandy on 6 June 1944, they are ordered on a daring mission behind enemy lines to find and rescue a Private James Ryan. His three brothers have been killed in action on the same day, and the secretary of war back home in America decides that the last remaining Ryan boy should be brought home to his mother. After the opening scenes (which contain some of the most horrific and poignant sights ever filmed), the remaining two hours of the movie portray the rescue mission itself, as Miller's team eventually finds Ryan.

Spielberg's film is a masterpiece. This is not just an action movie. This is a film with different layers of meaning. It is, in fact, a thinking person's war film. Take, for example, the *motif* of the cross. Crosses and crucifixes appear throughout *Saving Private Ryan*. The first and the last scenes of the film are shot in a war cemetery, where the now elderly James Ryan goes to pay his respects at the cross with Captain Miller's name on it. This is an example of the device known as *inclusio*, or 'ring composition', which I mentioned in chapter 1. The beginning and the end of the film focuses on a man kneeling before a cross. During the rest of the film crosses keep reappearing. One of captain Miller's men, a sharp shooter from Tennessee called Jackson (acted by Barry Pepper), kisses the crucifix around his neck before he aims at the enemy. As he prepares to shoot, he quotes Scripture and prays. You cannot get away from the cross in *Saving Private Ryan*.

Why is the plot of this film punctuated with images of the cross? The answer is because the cross is the pre-eminent image of salvation in the history of the world. This film is about salvation. It is about the value of one person's life (often a theme in Spielberg's works) and the lengths people will go to in order to save a single life. Keep in mind that this film is called *Saving Private Ryan*. The word 'saving' is a present participle. It denotes a process of actions that revolve around the theme and purpose of salvation. Spielberg has cleverly woven images of salvation into a film about people who give their lives to save others. When you recall that Stephen Spielberg is a Jew – and that the cross is, as Paul wrote, a stumbling block to the Jewish people – this fact is even more remarkable.

But it is precisely at this point that we have to recognise a paradox. Images of the cross point to the gospel or good news that Jesus died in our place that we might be forgiven. In other words, the cross is a reminder that salvation has been won for us at Calvary and that we no longer have to strive to gain God's acceptance through works. The cross reminds us that, as the saying goes, salvation is free even though it is not cheap.

At the end of *Saving Private Ryan*, Ryan is indeed saved. But he is saved at a price. Most of Miller's team is killed during the journey to the place where Ryan is located. Towards the end of the film, Miller himself sits dying on a bridge. The enemy has been defeated and Private Ryan can now go home. But Miller's life is ebbing away. Ryan stands before Miller and Miller, with his final breath, asks Ryan to lean towards him. As he does so, Miller just whispers the two words, 'Earn this.'[2]

'Earn this!' I remember when I watched this film in the cinema. I was absolutely captivated by the entire story. I was wholly on the side of Captain Miller, and my heart was going out to him as he gave up his life for Private Ryan. I could not help thinking of Jesus, who said that there is no greater love than this, that a man lay down his life for his friends. But when Miller said the words, 'Earn this', I felt the strongest urge to jump out of my seat and shout out, 'Salvation isn't earned! It's free. What on earth are you saying?'

You will be relieved to hear that I did not actually do this. But what a stunning contradiction lies at the heart of this film! On the one hand Spielberg keeps reminding us of the free gift of salvation won for us at Calvary. On the other hand, he ends his film with the opposite message – that salvation, achieved at a huge cost, has to be earned. Spielberg simply cannot help reverting back to the doctrine that salvation has to be gained through works. No wonder the film ends with the elderly Ryan in a war cemetery racked with guilt and saying to his wife, 'Tell me I'm a good man. Tell me if you think I've earned it.'³ Guilt – whether it is survival guilt or religious guilt – persistently torments the person for whom salvation is not perceived as free.

Salvation and solidarity

Jesus said that he came to seek and to save the lost (Luke 19:10). The whole purpose of his mission was to save sinners. Someone has said that if our greatest need had been for money, God would have sent us an economist. If our greatest need had been for knowledge, God would have sent us an educationalist. If our greatest need had been for conservation, God would have sent us an environmentalist. But our greatest need was for forgiveness, so God sent us a Saviour. As the Apostle Paul wrote: 'Here is a trustworthy saying that deserves full acceptance: Christ Jesus came into the world to save sinners' (1 Timothy 1:15).

It may seem strange that this very obvious point about salvation might need repeating. However, in recent decades, there has been a subtle shift in people's understanding of the cross, particularly in the West. During the Reformation the church saw the cross as a manifestation of the grace by which we are saved. The cross was inextricably bound up with our salvation from sin and the rallying cry was *sola fide*, 'only by faith'. From the Reformers on, salvation consisted of faith in the finished work of the cross. Paul said it all in Ephesians 2:8–9: 'For it is by grace you have been saved, through faith – and this not from yourselves, it is the gift of God – not by works, so that no one can boast.'

Until the twentieth century, salvation was therefore the pre-eminent concept for understanding and actualising the benefits of the cross. However, the twentieth century was marred by appalling suffering, stemming from two world wars, the holocaust, numerous international conflicts, terrorism and crime. In the light of all this horror, it is hardly surprising that theologians started to embrace an alternative model for understanding the cross. They stopped seeing the cross exclusively in terms of salvation and started to regard it as God's expression of his solidarity with suffering creation.[4] This paradigm shift from salvation to solidarity occurred (significantly) in the aftermath of World War Two, when theologians tried to develop what is called a 'theodicy' – an answer to the question, 'How can a loving God allow suffering?'

During the post-war years, a 'crucified God' theology began to emerge.[5] Put simply, this stated that God does not stand aloof from human suffering but that he himself suffers with us. The classical Greek idea of God's *apatheia* or remoteness is replaced by a vision of the New Testament revelation of God's *synpatheia* or identification with the world's victims. God has demonstrated his solidarity with those who suffer by experiencing rejection, abandonment, torture and death in the person of his Son. When human beings suffer, God suffers too. The cross discloses the extraordinary truth that pain and death have been experienced by the second person of the Trinity. As Charles Wesley put it, ' 'Tis mystery all, the immortal dies!'[6] From the solidarity point of view, the cross reveals once and for all a suffering rather than an apathetic God. The writer to the Hebrews sums it up as follows: 'For we do not have a high priest who is unable to sympathise with our weaknesses, but we have one who has been tempted in every way, just as we are – yet was without sin' (Hebrews 4:15).

What are we to make of this solidarity view? I well remember reading Corrie Ten Boom's book *The Hiding Place* as a young Christian. I was profoundly impacted by her story of how she and her sister Betsie were sent to a death camp for sheltering Jews in Holland. I remember reading how these two sisters kept hope alive in the lives of their fellow inmates by turning their sleeping quarters into a secret place of prayer. I also remember vividly Betsie's instructions before she died, 'Corrie, tell the world there is no pit of suffering so deep that Jesus Christ is not deeper still.' It is hard to imagine a more eloquent expression of a suffering God theology than this. This understanding of the cross is therefore perfectly permissible.

Yet, at the same time, we cannot allow solidarity to usurp salvation as the premier vision for the cross of Christ. If we do away with salvation, we do away with the very identity of the one whose name means 'Salvation'. The solidarity view of the cross is not an alternative to the salvation view. It is a view that can legitimately be expressed, but in a secondary role. Yes, the cross highlights God's identification with those who endure trials and tribulations. But the cross also primarily highlights the enormous cost God was prepared to bear in order to save us from our sins. We may feel that Captain John Miller paid a great price to cross an ocean in order to save one man. But God went to far greater lengths than this, spanning the vast distance between heaven and earth in order to rescue the whole world from the domination of Satan and the grip of sin. For this reason we cannot allow the salvation view of the cross to disappear through neglect. It must be restored to its rightful place. As Tom Smail has written: 'We cannot be true to the gospel unless we also give full weight to its claim that the primary meaning of the death of Jesus is that through it we are delivered from our sins.'[7]

The order of salvation

It is at this point that we must begin to look again at the relationship between the work of the Spirit and the work of the cross. In Part One we looked at the relationship between the work of the Spirit and the *fact* of the cross. In Part Two we are going to be looking at the relationship between the work of the Spirit and the *fellowship* of the cross in our own lives. Put another way, our main concern from now on will be the different ways in which the Holy Spirit applies the finished work of the cross to our lives as believers.

In the New Testament, crucifixion is both something done *for* us (by Jesus) and something done *in* us (by the Holy Spirit). On the one hand, what God accomplished at Calvary he accomplished objectively. As Paul says, 'God was reconciling the world to himself in Christ' (2 Corinthians 5:19). The cross is therefore in itself a perfect and all-sufficient sacrifice. It does not in any way depend on us. On the other hand, this salvation must be actualised subjectively in our lives. The cross has to become an experience as well as an event. As Gordon Fee puts it: 'Salvation in Christ is not simply a theological truth, predicated on God's prior action and the historical work of Christ. Salvation is an experienced reality, made so by the person of the Spirit coming into our lives.'[8]

How does God apply salvation to our lives? Clearly, we

do not earn God's salvation. Captain Miller's statement, 'Earn this', is a curse that has oppressed the minds of human beings from time immemorial. No one has ever been able to earn God's salvation. From our side we were utterly helpless, lost and depraved because of sin. No amount of good works could ever have earned our acquittal and acceptance in heaven. But God took the initiative from his side, as it were, to help the helpless. He did what humanity could not do. He provided a way out of sin through the death of his one and only Son. When we needed it most, the Father sent his Son to deliver us from the curse of the 'earn this' mentality. As Paul put it: 'When the time had fully come, God sent his Son, born of a woman, born under law, to redeem those under law, that we might receive the full rights of sons' (Galatians 4:4–5).

From these words we can see that our redemption involves the work of the Father and the work of the Son. The Father shows his love for us by sending his Son. The Son shows his love for us by dying on the cross. The great plan of redemption therefore involves both the Father and the Son. But it also involves the work of the Holy Spirit. God does not call out from the cross, 'This is what I have done for you; now earn this.' Rather, as we choose to believe the message of the cross, God sends his Spirit, who is the fire of his love, into our hearts. As Paul says in the verse after the passage just quoted: 'Because you are sons, God sent the Spirit of his Son into our hearts, the Spirit who calls out, "*Abba*, Father"' (Galatians 4:6). So the work of salvation not only involves the Father (who gives his Son) and the Son (who gives his life) but also the Holy Spirit (who makes these ancient facts a burning, life-changing reality for us today). The Trinity as a whole was involved in the great work of salvation. The Father devises the *plan* of salvation. The Son does the *work* of salvation.

The *application* of our salvation is the unique work of the person of the Holy Spirit. It is through the work of the Spirit that the benefits of Calvary are actualised in our lives.

The application of salvation is a dynamic process of events involving the work of the Spirit and our own response to the message of the cross. Over the centuries, theologians have described the progression of these saving events as the *ordo salutis*, or 'order of salvation'. This order consists of a number of critical components, all of which need to be examined because they involve an interplay of the work of the Spirit and the work of the cross.[9] While there is some variety in the different descriptions of the 'order of salvation', the essential elements are:

1. Calling – God's work of revelation in the hearts of the lost, through which he calls out for relationship
2. Conviction – the recognition that we have wandered from God, and the experience of godly sorrow over sin
3. Justification – believing with all one's heart in the work of the cross, resulting in God's declaration, 'Pardoned and acquitted!'
4. Regeneration – being born again through the power of the Spirit and receiving new life, the life of the age to come
5. Adoption – the Holy Spirit assuring us that God is our Father and that we are his children.

All five of these elements concern the beginnings of salvation. Keep in mind that salvation is a process as well as a crisis. In other words, it does not only involve the critical chain of events outlined above. It also involves a progressive work that continues throughout our earthly lives. However, in this chapter I am exclusively focusing on how we enter into our salvation. I want to show how the Spirit applies the work of the cross in each of the five areas above. In chapter 6, I will be looking at the Christian life in its entirety, stressing the way in which the cross must be applied to our lives daily (the process known as sanctification). In the present context, I want to confine myself to the beginnings of salvation.

1. The call of God

Throughout Scripture, God is described as one who calls us to hear, obey and follow him. In Deuteronomy 28:9–11, Moses reminds the people of Israel that they have been called by God, and that they will remain within the protection and privilege of that calling if they are obedient to God:

> The LORD will establish you as his holy people, as he promised you on oath, if you keep the commands of the LORD your God and walk in his ways. Then all the peoples on earth will see that you are *called* [my italics] by the name of the LORD, and they will fear you.

In the Gospels, Jesus called many people to follow him. The Apostle Peter speaks about the church as a chosen people, a royal priesthood, a holy nation, God's own people, who have been '*called* out of darkness into his wonderful light' (1 Peter 2:9, my italics). Likewise, the Apostle Paul says to the Corinthian believers that they were '*called . . .* into fellowship with his Son' (1 Corinthians 1:9, my italics). He encourages the Ephesian church members to live a life 'worthy of the *calling* you have received' (Greek literally: 'worthy of the calling of which you were called', Ephesians 4:1, my italics). Most revealing of all, Paul states in 2 Timothy 1:8–9 (Greek literally) that 'God saved us and called us with a holy calling.' Here Paul explicitly connects salvation and what is known as 'effectual calling' – the call that is effective for salvation.

How does God save and call us? The principal way in which God has chosen to save sinners is through the preaching of the good news that Christ died for our sins and that he rose again and is therefore alive today. Paul shows the connection between preaching the gospel and effectual calling in 2 Thessalonians 2:13–14:

> We ought always to thank God for you, brothers loved by the Lord, because from the beginning God chose you to be saved through the sanctifying work of the Spirit and through belief in the truth. *He called you to this through our gospel* [my italics], that you might share in the glory of our Lord Jesus Christ.

It is important not to be distracted by issues of predestination at this point. The main thing is to notice Paul's comment that the believers in Thessalonica were called to salvation 'through our gospel'. As this gospel was faithfully, clearly and accurately presented, the Holy Spirit worked in the hearts of the lost, calling them to salvation. Preaching the gospel is therefore the principal, divinely ordained means by which people hear the call of God upon their lives. This has been true throughout church history and is still true today.

I will never forget one particular incident that highlighted this. I was asked to preach at a wedding in an ancient village church in Oxfordshire. As the guests arrived, they parked their very expensive cars and walked into the church. In my heart, I did not sense much faith that day. The church building looked like a monument to a dead religion and the people looked as though they had absolutely no need of anything. Worse still, I did not sense the power of God in my life at all that day. I felt empty and weak.

However, I preached a very ordinary sermon, and towards the end I mentioned the cross, talking in very simple terms about the life-changing impact of Christ's sacrificial love at Calvary. To my amazement, a lady sent me a letter three months later in which she wrote the following:

> I'd like you to know that your sermon at the wedding was the clinching moment in my becoming a Christian. In the months prior to the wedding, I had been going through a difficult time after experiencing miscarriages and the realisation that I couldn't have any more children. Anyway, through the blackness of those days I had a vision of Christ on the cross, although it wasn't actually saying anything to me.
>
> When you ended your sermon with, 'Love is . . . Christ on the cross', it finally came home to me, the enormity of his sacrifice; he became real for the first time in my life. Since then, my life has turned around and I feel so much more at peace with myself. . . . I'm revelling in all the discoveries and challenges which come with a Christian life. So thank you; the Spirit was working through you that day!

This is a fascinating example of the sovereign way in which the Father calls people for salvation. Notice something about the preacher first of all. The effectiveness of the gospel message was not dependent upon his feelings. The gospel of the cross is the 'power of God for the salvation of everyone who believes' (Romans 1:16). Every time we speak about the cross, God's power is at work irrespective of what we ourselves sense or see. Even if the context looks depressing and the people look rebellious, the Holy Spirit is still moving, revealing the work of the cross to unbelievers. As the woman said in her letter, the Spirit was working through me that day even though I was unaware of the fact. God's power was at work in my weakness.

Secondly, notice something about the woman who received salvation. She wrote that she had already seen a vision of Christ on the cross even before she heard the gospel. Here again we see the sovereignty of God at work. The Holy Spirit was already revealing the work of the cross before she heard the message. An unbeliever received prophetic revelation concerning Calvary even before the gospel was preached! This is truly God's grace at work; God calling the lost before they hear the gospel. Here is the most striking example of this I have heard recently:

For twenty years, the inhabitants of a Cambodian village worshipped 'the God who hung on a cross' – without ever knowing Jesus. The village in Khampong Thom province was controlled by the Khmer Rouge, but the people have since readily accepted the gospel, almost as though they had been waiting for it. An old woman told how God protected the people from being massacred along with 1.7 million others in the 1970s. They were forced to dig their own graves while soldiers prepared to execute them. Desperate, they called on all the gods which came to mind to help them. Some prayed to Buddha, some to other gods, while the old woman prayed to 'the God who hung on a cross'. As they cowered on the ground, waiting for the shots, she recounts that she saw a vision of the cross, then heard a voice telling them that they would be saved: 'None but I can save you', the voice said. When they opened their eyes, the soldiers had vanished. Since that time, the villagers have prayed to the God who rescued them, but they knew nothing about Christ till a missionary visited the area and preached to them. They now know Jesus by name and have started a church. The old woman is so happy; she had waited for this day for twenty years.[10]

The Spirit reveals the cross to sinners *before* they hear the gospel. The Spirit reveals the cross to sinners as they hear the gospel. Only the Holy Spirit can bring this kind of illumination to darkened minds. Paul says that Satan, the god of this age, has blinded the minds of unbelievers. But it is God who says, 'Let light shine out of darkness' (2 Corinthians 4:4,6).

2. The conviction of sin

Wayne Grudem writes of the calling of God that it is 'a kind of "summons" from the King of the universe and it has such power that it brings about the response that it asks for in people's hearts'.[11] What exactly is this response which the call of God requires?

First and foremost, it is repentance. Repentance may be defined as a godly sorrow over sin, leading to a change of mind, a change of heart, and a change of behaviour. Repentance is not just saying sorry. It is a complete change of direction, a U-turn from disobedience to obedience.

True repentance is characterised by the experience of 'conviction'. In the first stages of salvation, a person hears the Father's call upon their life as the cross is revealed. As this occurs, the sinner recognises with profound anguish their unbelief and unrighteousness. All this is in fulfilment of Jesus' promise that the Holy Spirit would convict the world of its guilt in regard to sin and righteousness and judgment (John 16:8–11). The experience of conviction is accordingly a sign of the work of the Spirit. As the work of the cross comes into focus before their eyes, sinners see with dreadful clarity their dire need for forgiveness. If the sin of the world had necessitated such drastic action on God's part, then it must be serious indeed.

Most often this experience of conviction occurs as the

message of the cross is preached. The most striking example of this is in Acts 2, where Peter preaches the gospel and three thousand people are 'cut to the heart' (Acts 2:37). We may note that Peter does not shrink at all from saying to his hearers that *they* put Jesus on the cross. At the very start of his message he says, 'You, with the help of wicked men, put him to death by nailing him to the cross' (Acts 2:23). At the end he declares, 'Therefore let all Israel be assured of this: God has made this Jesus, whom you crucified, both Lord and Christ' (Acts 2:36). The crowds, hearing that Jesus, the sinless Messiah, was violently killed but is now risen, are cut to the heart and ask, 'What shall we do?' Peter's first response is to tell them to repent. The good news is that there can be forgiveness of sins. But first there has to be a turning away from our sin in heartfelt conviction.

It is recorded that the great preacher Charles Spurgeon was once asked to speak in the Crystal Palace in London. He went with a friend to try out the acoustics the day before. He went on to the platform while his friend listened from different parts of the great auditorium. Mounting the stage, the preacher declared in a loud, booming voice, 'Behold! The Lamb of God, that taketh away the sin of the world!' He repeated that statement several times before he and his friend left, happy that Spurgeon's voice projection was right for the venue. What both men had failed to notice was that a workman had been in the auditorium, doing some last minute repairs on part of the roof. That man went home from his work that day with a deep conviction of sin and, as a result of this one statement alone, gave his life to Jesus.

Conviction of sin is the work of the Spirit. It accompanies, confirms and follows the preaching of the cross. As with the matter of calling, however, the Holy Spirit sometimes produces conviction in people while they are not in church and nowhere near a preacher. This is especially true in seasons of revival.

My own story is perhaps helpful in this regard.[12] I received salvation during an extraordinary season of revival at my school. Scores of teenagers were giving their lives to Jesus Christ, but I held out. Then, one night, while I was walking down a road called Kingsgate Street, I suddenly felt cut to the heart. I had been far away from God, resisting his overtures of love. Now I knew that I was a sinner, that I had to respond to God's call upon my life, and that there was an urgency about it. I therefore ran to the home of a Christian teacher and fell upon the floor of his front room, whereupon I was led through a prayer of repentance and commitment, and found peace with God.

For me personally, it was not during the preaching of a sermon that I fell under conviction, nor was it in a church building. The Holy Spirit preached the message that night, and a road in Winchester was the church. In fact, that street I was walking down became Kingsgate Street spiritually; it became the gate through which I met the king of kings.

The second stage of the 'order of salvation' is therefore conviction. This is the work of the Spirit disclosing to our hearts our desperate need for forgiveness. The principal means by which this occurs is through the preaching of the gospel of the crucified and risen Jesus. But it can also occur through the direct intervention of the Holy Spirit in our lives.

3. Justification by faith

Third on the list of the *ordo salutis* is 'justification by faith'. Here we move to the language of the law courts. The word translated justification could equally well be translated 'acquittal'. Justification is accordingly the act by which

God acquits us so that we can stand before his holy presence in the sure knowledge that we are pardoned.

Our justification is based solely on the finished work of the cross. Grace is the key here. We did not deserve to be acquitted, but in Christ, the judge as it were has left his high seat, stood in the dock on our behalf, and taken the punishment in our place. As Paul so beautifully puts it,

> You see, at just the right time, when we were still powerless, Christ died for the ungodly. Very rarely will anyone die for a righteous man, though for a good man someone might possibly dare to die. But God demonstrates his own love for us in this: While we were still sinners, Christ died for us.
>
> Romans 5:6–8

As a result of this priceless act of substitution, we are justified. The verb 'justify' means 'to declare righteous'. As a result of Calvary, God declares that we are now just or righteous in his sight. This declaration involves two astounding revelations of God's love. First of all, the Father declares that he no longer counts our sins against us (2 Corinthians 5:19). Rodman Williams describes the situation thus:

> Although they be as a great mountain, though they be a vast number, though they be as black as night, God does not impute, does not count, them against us. We cannot pretend that sins are not there – and surely God makes no such pretence – but they are not charged to our account. We may shudder at some thought of a heavenly account book, with column upon column of entries against us, and sense the horror of God's coming condemnation. But, praise God, the record is clear; there are no such entries. Somehow, somewhere, they have all been removed.[13]

So the Father first of all declares that he does not impute our sins against us. The sinner who experiences conviction and offers repentance finds forgiveness of sins. Secondly, justification means that God imputes to us the righteousness of his Son. Wayne Grudem writes: 'When we say that God *imputes* Christ's righteousness to us it means that God *thinks* of Christ's righteousness as belonging to us. . . . He "reckons" it to our account.[14]

Christ becomes our righteousness (1 Corinthians 1:30). Once we are 'in Christ', we begin to participate in Christ's righteousness. We are covered, as it were, with the robe of his righteousness (Isaiah 61:10). When God looks at us he therefore sees the righteousness of his Son. What amazing grace!

What must we do to enter into this standing before God? The answer is, 'Only believe'. Certainly this great grace cannot be enjoyed through works. It is by faith alone that we are reckoned righteous by God. It is certainly not by any righteousness of our own that we stand acquitted before the judge of all. Rather, by humbly trusting that all our sins have been paid for at Calvary we are justified and acquitted (Romans 3:28). So faith is required as well as repentance if we are to be saved. In the place of desperation, as we acknowledge that we are in dire need of forgiveness, we come to believe that Christ died for our sins. We start to trust that everything necessary for our salvation was accomplished once and for all at Calvary. As we do so, the long night of restlessness comes to an end. The peace we have been searching for throughout our entire lives floods our weary souls. We are able to declare with the Apostle Paul, 'Since we have been justified through faith, we have peace with God through our Lord Jesus Christ' (Romans 5:1).

Justification is therefore grounded on the finished work

of the cross. What, then, of the work of the Spirit? How does this relate to justification? We need to understand that saving faith is not merely an intellectual assent to certain doctrinal truths. It is a matter of the heart. Paul says that a person believes with their heart and so is justified (Romans 10:10). How can a human heart respond in trust and commitment to the living God? The answer is by the Holy Spirit. Paul says in Romans 5:5 that God has poured out his love into our hearts by the Holy Spirit. What does 'his love' refer to? Does it mean that God poured out his love for us? Or does it mean that he ignites a fire in our hearts that enables us to love him? Personally, I believe it is the latter. As we choose of our own free will to believe, the Holy Spirit gives to our hearts a passionate love of God, a joy in receiving our salvation, and a sense of profound *shalom* or peace. As we believe and trust in the finished work of the cross, the Holy Spirit floods our souls – our minds, hearts and wills – with the certain knowledge that we stand acquitted in the law courts of heaven.

No conversion has been written about more than John Wesley's. His experience in 1738 is key to understanding what I am writing about here:

> In the evening I went very unwillingly to a society in Aldersgate Street, where one was reading Luther's preface to the Epistle to the Romans. About a quarter before nine, while he was describing the change which God works in the heart through faith in Christ, I felt my heart strangely warmed. I felt I did trust in Christ, Christ alone for salvation; and an assurance was given me that He had taken away *my* sins, even *mine*, and saved me from the law of sin and death.[15]

Here the work of the Spirit and the work of the cross are united. As Wesley heard Martin Luther's great testimony of justification by faith not by works, Wesley experienced a burning heart. The fire of God's love ignited a sense of trust and confidence that he had not possessed before. He knew in his own experience the benefits of the finished work of the cross. It was the Holy Spirit who applied the truth that Wesley was now acquitted and righteous.

4. Rebirth by Spirit

Regeneration is a miraculous moment in the order of salvation. Regeneration means literally the process of being born again. Just as birth brought us physical life in the natural realm, so rebirth brings us new life in the spiritual realm. Having repented and believed, we now stand forgiven before God. But there is more to come. Having been called, convicted and justified, we are now born again by the Holy Spirit. A profound inward change occurs in our lives which is exclusively the work of the Spirit. Thus John says in his Gospel that those who believe in Jesus are born of God. This spiritual rebirth is not the result of any human initiative but the result of the work of God (John 1:12–13). It is specifically the work of the Holy Spirit, because Jesus says that we are born 'of the Spirit' (John 3:5–8). We are therefore passive in the matter of regeneration. Just as we play no active part in our own physical birth, so we play no active part in our rebirth.

Regeneration is an instantaneous, unique and mysterious event. It is instantaneous because the Holy Spirit brings new life to our dead spirit in an instant. It is unique because it only happens once (just as physical birth only happens once). It is mysterious because it is entirely the result of the supernatural, life-changing activity of God's Holy Spirit. As Jesus said: 'You should not be surprised at my saying, "You must be born again." The wind blows wherever it pleases. You hear its sound, but you cannot tell where it comes from or where it is going. So it is with everyone born of the Spirit' (John 3:7–8). So rebirth is essential for salvation. As Jesus said, we *must* be born again if we are to see and to enter the kingdom of God (John 3:3–5). Regeneration is not an option but a necessity. It is the moment when we receive the promised gift of the Spirit and begin to walk in newness of life.

In this we see again the glorious interplay of the work of the Spirit and the work on the cross. Ezekiel had prophesied a day when God would put a new spirit within his people. As we have already seen in chapter 3, this would come through the new covenant established through the blood of Christ shed on the cross. Once we choose to believe in the finished work of the cross, we can receive the life-giving Spirit and start all over again, no longer living for ourselves but living for God. Believing is therefore the key to receiving. As Paul clearly states in Galatians 3:2, we receive the gift of the Holy Spirit as we believe the message of Christ crucified.

We might put it this way. In the life of Jesus we see how the Spirit leads to the cross, and then how the cross leads to the Spirit. In our own lives, a similar process also occurs. The Spirit leads us to the cross as we hear God's call and as we experience conviction. But the cross also leads us to the Spirit. As we believe in the finished work of the cross, the living water of God's Spirit begins to vitalise our spirits and flood our hearts. The Spirit leads us to the cross in revelation. The cross leads us to the Spirit in regeneration. We cannot do without either of these if we are to enter our salvation.

5. Adoption into God's family

We come now to the final indispensable requirement in the order of salvation, the experience of spiritual adoption. Since I have written a whole book on this subject I will say here far less than I could.[16]

Spiritual adoption is the process by which we enter into the confident assurance that God is our Father and that we are his children. This experience of spiritual adoption only occurs after we have chosen to believe in the finished work of the cross. As we believe the gospel, we receive the new life of the Spirit. This Spirit is the Spirit of adoption. Thus Paul says to those who are already believers, 'You did not receive a spirit that makes you a slave again to fear, but you received the Spirit of sonship [adoption]. And by him we cry, "*Abba*, Father" (Romans 8:15). In Galatians 4:6, this thought is elaborated. It is because we have become sons (through repentance, faith and rebirth), that God sends the Spirit into our hearts, the Spirit who calls out, '*Abba*, Father.'

I have argued in my book, *From Orphans to Heirs*, that the legal image of salvation has dominated Western Christianity since the Reformation. Our natural tendency has been to see God as judge and salvation as a matter of acquittal. However, the Holy Spirit wants us to see a far more glorious picture of the love of God (Ephesians 3:17–19). As we begin to comprehend the extraordinary grace of adoption, we see that this holy judge is also a glorious Father. We see that our salvation is not just a matter of hearing the declaration 'Pardoned and acquitted'. It is also a matter of hearing the Father declaring, 'You are my child, my beloved. With you I am well pleased!'

It is my belief that the Reformers gave us an incomplete picture. They enabled us to see that we are justified before a fearsome judge but they did not enable us to see that we are intimately loved, accepted and embraced by an affectionate Father. A key reason why this might have happened may have been Martin Luther's poor relationship with his own father. As he wrote: 'I have difficulty praying the Lord's Prayer because whenever I say "Our Father", I think of my own father who was hard, unyielding and relentless. I cannot help but think of God that way.'[17]

This is a most revealing comment and highlights why Luther and his followers did not give the doctrine of adoption its rightful place. However, if we neglect spiritual adoption in the order of salvation, we pay a great price. Believers will always have a tendency to revert to slavery and fear. The Spirit of God must be allowed to apply the work of the cross in a relational and not just a legal way. If people are to be properly initiated into the kingdom of God, then they need to know that they are welcome in the living room, not just acquitted in the court room.

Fullness and faith

So there is a very rich interplay between the work of the Spirit and the work of the cross in the order of salvation. The Spirit reveals the cross as the Father calls out to us for relationship. The Spirit takes us to the cross as we cry out to the Father under conviction of sin. The Spirit applies the cross as we experience the amazing grace of sins forgiven and righteousness received. The Spirit flows from the cross as we receive the life of the age to come in the experience of regeneration. Finally, the Spirit personalises the cross as we become the adopted children of our Father in heaven.

Salvation is therefore a gift to be received, not a trophy to be earned. The 'Earn this' mentality typified by the message of *Saving Private Ryan* has no place in a true biblical understanding of salvation. Yet many Christians succumb to the devil's attempts to make them slaves again to a performance orientation. This tendency to revert to the bondage of legalism was something that Paul came across frequently. When we read a letter like Galatians it is quite evident that Paul is confronting Jewish Christians who have slipped back into reliance on works. It is particularly sad that these deluded people were teaching others that the key to the Spirit-filled life was dependent upon obedience to Torah (including circumcision, Sabbath regulations, and the like). All this made it necessary for Paul to say words that demonstrate tough love in Galatians 3:1–5:

> You foolish Galatians! Who has bewitched you? Before your very eyes Jesus Christ was clearly portrayed as crucified. I would like to learn just one thing from you: Did you receive the Spirit by observing the law, or by believing what you heard? Are you so foolish? After beginning with the Spirit, are you now trying to attain your goal by human effort? Have you suffered so much for nothing – if it really was for nothing? Does God give you his Spirit and work miracles among you because you observe the law, or because you believe what you heard?

Paul's words here are of critical importance in any study of the relationship between the Spirit and the cross.[18] Here Paul states without equivocation that faith is the path to fullness. More specifically, Paul clearly teaches that believing in the cross is the key to receiving the Spirit.

Returning to Spielberg's movie, it is a shame that Captain Miller so brutally subverts the message of salvation suggested by all the images of the cross throughout *Saving Private Ryan*. Had Miller refrained from using the word 'earn' as he died, it is quite possible that the final scene of the movie would have portrayed the elderly Ryan moved by gratitude rather than wracked by guilt. That would have been a more wholesome and, dare I say it, a more loving vision of sacrifice than the one Spielberg provides. In a scene where Ryan kneels amidst an ocean of white crosses, that would also have been a more fitting vision.

In the final analysis, we simply cannot earn our salvation. Gerrit Gustafson is right on the mark when he says,

> Only by grace can we enter,
> Only by grace can we stand;
> Not by our human endeavour,
> But by the blood of the Lamb.[19]

We cannot achieve salvation through being good or doing good works. Entering into the Spirit-filled life can never be achieved through the keeping of religious rules and regulations. The gift of salvation and the gift of the Spirit are grounded in God's grace, and they are received not by works but by believing in the finished work of the cross. In the matter of salvation, as in so many other areas, we must keep the cross and the Spirit together.

Chapter 5

MISSION AND MIRACLES

For I resolved to know nothing while I was with you except Jesus Christ and him crucified. I came to you in weakness and fear, and with much trembling. My message and my preaching were not with wise and persuasive words, but with a demonstration of the Spirit's power . . .

1 Corinthians 2:2–4

The answer of God to all the problems of human nature lie in two inseparable divine operations: the work of the cross, and the work of the Holy Spirit.

Tom Marshall, *Free Indeed*[1]

Several years ago a Sunday morning meeting was in progress at a local church in Uganda. As the pastor was speaking, a three-year-old girl walked up to him, pulled on his trouser leg, and asked for the microphone. The pastor gave it to her and the girl started to say, 'Jesus saves! Jesus heals! Jesus delivers!' She paused. Then she spoke again,

'Jesus saves! Jesus heals! Jesus delivers!' Again she paused. Then again, 'Jesus saves! Jesus heals! Jesus delivers!' As she spoke this third time, people in the church started to weep over their sins and cry out for forgiveness. Others started shouting, 'I can see!', 'I can hear!', 'I can walk!' Others poured forward to be set free from all manner of spiritual oppression.

The most extraordinary thing about this story is the fact that the little girl had died several weeks prior to this incident. She was about to be buried in the ground when the pastor prayed that she would be raised. Immediately she sat up, alive and well. When her pastor asked if she had seen or heard anything during the time between dying and being raised, she replied, 'Jesus came to me and told me to give this message, "Jesus saves! Jesus heals! Jesus delivers!"'

Proclamation and demonstration

Just occasionally you hear something that is so simple and yet so profoundly true you wonder why you never heard it put that way before. The message of this little girl comes into that category. If ever there was a creed that describes the king and the kingdom it has to be this. In these six words, we find the essence of Jesus' kingdom ministry: salvation, healing and deliverance.

Jesus began his ministry by quoting from the prophet Isaiah (Luke 4:18–19):

> The Spirit of the Lord is on me,
> because he has anointed me
> to preach good news to the poor.
> He has sent me to proclaim freedom for the prisoners
> and recovery of sight for the blind,

to release the oppressed,
to proclaim the year of the Lord's favour.

Jesus came first of all to preach the good news of God's compassion, mercy and forgiveness, extended to all. He came to save sinners. He came secondly to heal the sick, to bring recovery of the sight to the blind (among many other things). He came thirdly to bring deliverance – deliverance at a spiritual level (from evil spirits), and deliverance at a social level (from oppressive social structures). In short, he came to give forgiveness and freedom.

Jesus inaugurated and advanced the kingdom of God. The kingdom of God is God's rule on earth, pushing back the powers of darkness. The primary methodology for Jesus' kingdom ministry involved proclamation and demonstration. He preached the good news and he performed signs and wonders. As the two disciples on the Emmaus Road declared, Jesus was 'powerful in word and deed' (Luke 24:19). Through the authority of his preaching and the power of his miracles, the dynamic reign of almighty God was extended. Through words and through works, Jesus revealed his kingship and destroyed the work of the evil one – sin, sickness, demonisation, social oppression and death.

The apostles continued this methodology of words and works. Having been trained by the master over a period of three years, and having received authority and power, they spread the message that 'Jesus saves, heals and delivers', and backed up their message with signs and wonders. The Apostle Peter certainly continued to preach the message and to do the works of Jesus. In Acts 2 we find him preaching the gospel. In Acts 3 we find him healing the sick. Others also follow his lead. Philip is in many ways a classic example. He was used by God to advance the king-

dom throughout an entire Samaritan city. His methodology
was the same as Jesus, proclamation and demonstration:

> Philip went down to a city in Samaria and proclaimed the
> Christ there. When the crowds heard Philip and saw the mirac-
> ulous signs he did, they all paid close attention to what he
> said. With shrieks, evil spirits came out of many, and many
> paralytics and cripples were healed. So there was great joy in
> that city.
>
> Acts 8:5–8

Paul, having been miraculously converted, continues this
ministry of the word and the Spirit. He preaches the good
news and he also performs miracles. In fact, this combina-
tion of words and works characterised his entire ministry.
For this reason, he can say in Romans 15:18–19:

> I will not venture to speak of anything except what Christ has
> accomplished through me in leading the Gentiles to obey God
> by what I have said and done – by the power of signs and mir-
> acles, through the power of the Spirit. So from Jerusalem all
> the way around to Illyricum, I have fully proclaimed the
> gospel of Christ.

Notice Paul's emphasis on what he has *said* and *done*. The
kingdom was advanced in Paul's ministry through authoritative preaching of the gospel of Christ and through the
power of signs and miracles.

The message that 'Jesus saves, heals and delivers' is
therefore received in two ways, by hearing and by seeing.
This is why Jesus in his own ministry tells the disciples
of John the Baptist to tell their rabbi what they 'hear
and see'. They hear good news and they see miracles
(Matthew 11:4–5). Paul and others continue this way of
operating. In fact, Paul describes his normal ministry

procedure in 1 Corinthians 2:1–5:

> When I came to you, brothers, I did not come with eloquence
> or superior wisdom as I proclaimed to you the testimony
> about God. For I resolved to know nothing while I was with
> you except Jesus Christ and him crucified. I came to you in
> weakness and fear, and with much trembling. My message and
> my preaching were not with wise and persuasive words, but
> with a demonstration of the Spirit's power, so that your faith
> might not rest on men's wisdom, but on God's power.

Here we see most clearly the kingdom dynamic of proclamation and demonstration. Paul's desire was always to
preach the cross. But he knew that words alone were not
enough. As Paul states in 1 Corinthians 4:20, the kingdom
of God is not a matter of talk but of power. So Paul did not
depend on human eloquence. He trusted wholly in God,
recognising that it is not by human might or by human
strength that mountains are levelled but rather by God's
Holy Spirit (Zechariah 4:6). So demonstrations of the
Spirit's power accompanied the proclamation of the cross.

This brings us right back into the heart of our subject,
the relationship between the work of the Spirit and the
work of the cross. Once we have entered our salvation (see
chapter 4), we are now called to minister that salvation to
others. Having received so freely the amazing grace and
love of God, we are now motivated to give it away. Just as
we entered our salvation through the work of the cross and
the Spirit (the Spirit applying the benefits of the cross to
our lives), so we are now invited to continue combining
these two great works as we reach out to the lost. This
means giving a verbal testimony of the good news, and it
means praying for miracles. In short, we are to speak about
the work of the cross with demonstrations of the work of

the Spirit. People need to *hear* that Jesus saves, heals and delivers. But they also need to *see* these things.

1. Jesus saves!

The argument of this chapter is simple: the kingdom of God advances forcibly as the Holy Spirit applies the benefits of the finished work of the cross. These benefits include salvation, healing and deliverance. For a full picture, we must look at salvation first.

Since I have dealt with this topic in the last chapter, I will keep this brief. How does the Holy Spirit apply the benefits of the cross in the matter of personal salvation?

We need to go back to 1 Corinthians 2 to find the answer. In that chapter Paul continues his argument from chapter 1 where he has been speaking about the foolishness of the cross. The message of the cross appears foolish to the Hellenistic mind because it lacks wisdom, to the Hebraic mind because it lacks power.

For a person to understand the message of the cross, something more than rhetoric is therefore needed by the preacher, and something more than reason is required on the part of the sinner. Divine revelation is necessary. When Paul came to preach the message of Christ (having been) crucified, he therefore relied totally on the Holy Spirit for revelation. Rather than speaking the wisdom of words, he preferred to speak words of wisdom. At the same time, Paul depended on the Holy Spirit to do the convincing and the persuading. He knew only too well that he himself did not have the resources to bring his listeners to an understanding of the cross. Nor did he have the power to lead them to a changed life. The only thing that could bring a person to a saving knowledge of the Calvary love of God was a demonstration or 'proof' of the Spirit's power. It is for this reason that Paul continues after 1 Corinthians 2:1–5 to describe the work of the Spirit in revealing the secret wisdom of God.

What did Paul mean by a demonstration of the Spirit's power? I believe he was primarily referring to those moments when the Holy Spirit reveals the power of the cross to an unredeemed mind. When this happens, and a person crosses over from darkness to light, the greatest miracle of all has occurred. To be sure, Paul may also have been referring to signs and wonders such as physical healing miracles. What he writes elsewhere, especially in Romans 15:18–19, confirms this. But first and foremost Paul is alluding to that supernatural act of God in which the veil is removed from a person's mind, the blindness healed, and the light of the knowledge of the glory of God pours into their lives. When this happens, the Holy Spirit applies the work of the cross for the purpose of salvation.

Let us look at an example. Jonathan Edwards, in his account of the 1736 revival in Northampton, USA, describes a woman of about seventy years of age who suddenly came to a startling appreciation of the cross:[2]

Reading in the New Testament concerning Christ's suffering for sinners, she seemed to be astonished at what she read, as what was real and very wonderful, but quite new to her. At first, before she had time to turn her thoughts, she wondered within herself, that she had never heard of it before; but then immediately recollected herself, and thought she had often heard of it, and read it, but never till now saw it as real. She then cast in her mind how wonderful this was, that the Son of God should undergo such things for sinners, and how she had spent her time in ungratefully sinning against so good a God, and such a Saviour; though she was a person, apparently, of a very blameless and inoffensive life. And she was so overcome by those considerations that her nature was ready to fail under them: those who were about her, and knew not what was the matter, were surprised, and thought she was dying.

Edwards reports that this kind of revelation of 'the excellency and dying love of Jesus Christ' was very common during the revival. A few sentences after describing this woman's testimony, he writes: 'Some have been so overcome with a sense of the dying love of Christ to such poor, wretched and unworthy creatures, as to weaken the body.'

A little later he writes not only of failed bodily strength (probably manifested in swooning and falling over) but also of visions: 'Some, when they have been greatly affected with Christ's death, have at the same time a lively idea of Christ hanging upon the cross, and blood running from his wounds.'

That Edwards regarded such phenomena as demonstrations of 'the Spirit's power' is without dispute. In his essay, 'The Distinguishing Marks of a Work of the Spirit of God', he writes:

> When the operation is such as to raise their esteem of that Jesus was born of the Virgin, and was crucified without the gates of Jerusalem; and seems more to confirm and establish their minds in the truth of what the Gospel declares to us of his being the Son of God and the Saviour of men; it is a sure sign that it is from the Spirit of God.[3]

Such revelation must be evidence of the Spirit's power because the devil 'hates the story and doctrine of Christ's redemption'.

For a person to be truly saved, sin must be acknowledged with godly repentance, and forgiveness must be sought at the foot of the cross. Today in the church there is so much neglect of the reality of sin that those outside the church no longer know what they need saving from. Consequently, there are many 'life-enhancement' believers in the church – people who embrace Christianity as a path to achieving greater success in life. But this is a cultural distortion of the true gospel. A person only begins to experience their salvation as they come to the cross under the Spirit's work of revelation and conviction. Any other way undermines the great truth that 'Jesus saves!'

2. Jesus heals!

Salvation from sin is the primary benefit of the finished work of the cross, and it is by the power of the Spirit that this benefit is realised in our lives today.

Healing is also one of the blessings of the finished work of the cross. By 'healing' I am referring specifically to a powerful work of the Holy Spirit in which a disease or a disability is miraculously cured. The good news is that 'Jesus is the same yesterday and today and for ever' (Hebrews 13:8). He therefore still heals the sick today!

In October 1999, 400 delegates met for four days at St Andrew's, Chorleywood to pray for revival. One evening, some of the young people from the church laid hands on a chronically sick man. He had come to the conference barely able to walk. As two or three teenagers prayed for him he was instantly healed and then threw away his walking sticks in the process. At the meeting, we asked the man to produce doctor's verification of his healing and he subsequently did so. The report read that he had been ill with severe fibromyalgia for four years prior to the conference. His GP wrote that 'walking had been very difficult due to pain and stiffness in his legs and he has had to use a stick'. Another doctor wrote: 'There is no doubt that this man is severely disabled'.

As this man was prayed for at the conference he was healed. Since that time he has regained full mobility, and has found a new freedom in walking, running, climbing stairs, and so on. He wrote to me saying that his physical strength is improving all the time, with muscles that have been unused for four years becoming active once again.

A friend of his, an osteopath, wrote subsequently: 'When I saw him after the conference, he was completely free of the pain which had been his constant companion for so long, and was walking freely and without recourse to a stick.' The man himself, having been healed, told me that there were three beneficial results to his healing (in addition to his new found health and vigour). First, his whole faith, prayer life and relationship with God made massive strides forward. Secondly, his testimony had a remarkable impact on his local church, his friends, on unbelievers, and especially on the prisoners he visits as part of his outreach. Thirdly, he felt that the reason he had been set free from chronic sickness was to serve the Lord in some form of ministry, hopefully missionary work in Europe, as he speaks French, German and Dutch, and is learning Spanish.

And what of his doctor? After outlining the nature of his illness in a hand-written letter, the GP writes, 'There has been a sudden and dramatic improvement in his symptoms.'

Truly, as the three-year-old Ugandan girl declared, 'Jesus heals!'

In what sense, then, is healing a benefit of the cross? At this point we need to turn to a short passage in the Gospel of Matthew. The passage in question is in Matthew 8 (a chapter given over to healing miracles). After a man has been healed of leprosy in 8:1–4, and a centurion's servant has been healed of paralysis in 8:5–13, Matthew writes as follows: 'When Jesus came into Peter's house, he saw Peter's mother-in-law lying in bed with a fever. He touched her hand and the fever left her, and she got up and began to wait on him' (8:14–15).

After this, Peter's house becomes a house of healing. Matthew continues: 'When evening came, many who were demon-possessed were brought to him, and he drove out the spirits with a word and healed all the sick' (8:16). At this point, Matthew inserts a word of explanation: 'This was to fulfil what was spoken through the prophet Isaiah [in 53:4]: "He took up our infirmities and carried our diseases"' (8:17).

These words suggest that healing miracles of Jesus are a foretaste of the benefits of the cross.

We need to take care how we interpret this passage. It is around this text in Matthew 8:14–17 that some dangerous views about healing have been built up. Basically, the argument runs as follows. Isaiah's prophecy appears to suggest that Jesus bore our sicknesses as well as our sins at Calvary. Therefore, just as a sinner is automatically forgiven whenever they acknowledge their need of mercy, so a sick person is automatically healed whenever they acknowledge their need of healing. The key is therefore to name it and claim it. Confession and possession brings guaranteed healing.

Is this view sustainable? The answer is both 'yes' and 'no'. On the one hand, it is true that Matthew understands Isaiah's words literally. In his mind, the 'infirmities' and 'diseases' taken by the Messiah are understood as sicknesses.[4] The proof for that lies in the context of Matthew 8:17 which involves Jesus' healing people's bodies. This surely indicates that Matthew sees salvation in a holistic sense; as applying to our bodies as well as our souls.

On the other hand, the insistence that Jesus actually bore

our sicknesses on the cross is mistaken. Matthew's use of words in 8:17 does not permit this reading. In fact, it is vital to understand that Matthew changes the quotation from Isaiah 53:4 in one significant respect. In Isaiah 53:4 (the LXX or Greek version), we read: 'He carried (*pherei*) our infirmities and took our diseases.' Matthew, however, differs in respect to one word: 'He removed (*elaben*) our infirmities and took our diseases.' Matthew prefers the verb *remove* to the verb *carry*.[5] In the process, he portrays Jesus 'taking away' our sicknesses rather than 'bearing' them.

Now all this is more than a matter of mere semantics. What Jesus did on the cross was to deal the decisive and final blow against sin. In the process, Jesus defeated the power that lies behind human sickness. Here we need to remember that sickness was not originally a part of God's creation. It was sin that caused sickness to become a part of the created order. Tempted by the devil, Adam sinned and humanity fell from this pristine state of *shalom* or wholeness. When Adam sinned, humanity became alienated from God, and because God is the author of life, we became vulnerable to disease and death, which are the works of the devil. As Leon Morris puts it:

> In some way, Scripture seems to be saying, sickness came in at the Fall. It is to be understood not as part of God's original good creation, but as another part of the legacy of human sin. . . . Looked at in this way it is not at all surprising that Christ's atoning work should have as one of its effects a dealing with sickness, even if we do not see the full effects of that here and now.[6]

This brings us back to the cross. God sent his only Son into the world to restore what humanity had lost and to destroy the work of the evil one (1 John 3:8). Unlike the first Adam, the second Adam (Jesus) lives a life of obedience to death, even death on a cross. As such, he begins to reverse the work of the Fall. Sin and death were introduced into the world as a result of the first Adam's disobedience. Their power is now defeated through the obedience of the second Adam at Golgotha. The power of sickness is defeated as the crucified Messiah takes away the sin of the world. Thus it can truly be said that Jesus 'took our infirmities and removed our diseases'. Jesus dealt decisively with the problem of sin at Calvary, thereby making it possible for all manner of sickness and disease to be healed.

Having said that, the Bible clearly teaches that we will have to wait until the return of Christ before God creates a new Eden in which sickness and death will finally be eradicated. Until then, we live between the ages. We live in the present age, in which there is sickness and death. But we also live in the presence of the future, in which there is healing and life. Two consequences follow from this: people continue to become sick and to die, Christians included. This is an inevitable result of living in a world still affected by the first Adam's sin. However, those who have been born again live the life of the age to come. As a result they will sometimes see subjectively what has been achieved objectively on the cross – namely, the removal of sickness through the atoning death of Jesus Christ. Every time that occurs, the future breaks into human history ahead of time. The things of the end – including healing and even resurrection – are witnessed in the here and now.

Jesus still heals people miraculously today. Every time this happens, we can truly say that the kingdom of God has broken into the life of a sick person. However, the kingdom is 'not yet' as well as 'now'. This means that our prayers for physical healing will sometimes be greeted by the words 'not yet', sometimes 'now'. While God has covenanted to forgive sins every time a person repents, he has not covenanted to heal sicknesses every time a person asks for healing. Healing is accordingly a benefit of the finished work of the cross applied through the work of the Holy Spirit. But healing cannot and should not be regarded as immediate and automatic. We need to pray with faith for everyone to be healed, and yet at the same time allow God to be sovereign. Sometimes he has other plans.

One instance that brought this home to me personally involved a man called Steve who visited St Andrew's on Easter Sunday evening in 1999. Steve had cancer, having been diagnosed with a malignant melanoma about a year prior to this. The medics had given many assurances that the cancer would be cured, but in spite of this, Steve had deteriorated. By the time he came to the Easter Day celebration he was clearly very sick indeed.

Steve came in search of physical healing that night but, in the words of his girlfriend Sue, he found so much more. Steve was not a Christian but he did know the stories in the Bible about Jesus healing the sick. Sue had recently become a Christian and was praying hard for his recovery. So Steve came to us in hope that Jesus might heal him. On Easter Sunday evening, however, he heard the call of God on his life, repented of his sins, confessed his faith in Jesus, and was gloriously saved. From now on, whether he lived or died, it would be in the saving knowledge and love of Jesus.

Sadly, Steve deteriorated even more after this, even though some of our ministry team had fervently prayed for his healing. On a Friday morning several weeks later, he was in bed, unable to move. I will let Sue tell the rest of the story in her own words:

The cancer was all over his spine and trapping his nerves so he couldn't stand, he couldn't hold cups and do things that we take for granted. In the end he lost the power to speak and because he had cancer in his brain couldn't open his eyes. His vision was very, very poor.

On Friday, however, just a few minutes before he died, he opened his eyes wide and sat up in bed and grabbed hold of me. He said, 'Suzy, what's his name?' and I said 'Steve, his name is Jesus.' Steve was looking across my shoulder and he just said, 'Praise God, Praise God,' and then he went.

Sometimes, the answers to our most heartfelt prayers for physical healing are not what we would expect. On this occasion the answer was 'not yet'. Perhaps it was also 'not in the way you're asking'. Steve received salvation, and in a sense there is no higher form of healing than this, for this is the healing of a person's spirit, leading to eternal life with Jesus. For that reason, Sue could face Steve's death as an endless hope rather than a hopeless end. Just a few weeks later, she said these words, 'God's grace is sufficient. I thought before I was a Christian that when Steve went I would have nothing left to live for and I am here to tell you that Jesus is worth living for!'

3. Jesus delivers!

Everything I have written so far demonstrates that the Spirit applies the benefits of the cross in both salvation and healing. So far I have been writing about physical healing, but the truth is God is interested in healing the whole person. He is committed to seeing us healed not only in spirit, not only in our bodies (where he wills this), but also in our souls.

At times the New Testament seems to make a distinction between the spirit and the soul. Thus, the writer to the Hebrews says, 'The word of God is living and active.

Sharper than any double-edged sword, it penetrates even to dividing soul and spirit, joints and marrow; it judges the thoughts and attitudes of the heart' (Hebrews 4:12).

The differentiation between the spirit (*pneuma*) and the soul (*psyche*) is noticeable here. This would suggest that a human being is not a soul in a human body (the Hellenistic perspective) but rather a far more complex triunity of spirit, soul and body. This is further indicated by Paul's prayer in 1 Thessalonians 5:23 – 'May God himself, the God of peace, sanctify you through and through. May your whole spirit, soul and body be kept blameless at the coming of our Lord Jesus Christ.'

Here Paul exhorts every believer to keep their whole personhood in a state of constant holiness. This means watching over one's spirit (*pneuma*), soul (*psyche*) and body (*soma*) until the second coming. If a distinction is being made here between three different parts of a human person, then Paul is here transcending the Greek view of humans as dichotamous beings (soul and body).

Some people argue that Paul did not dissect the whole human personality into spirit, soul and body but that he is using words very loosely here. However, Paul is always careful with words. So is the Holy Spirit, who inspired Paul's words! Others argue that spirit and soul mean the same thing, and that they refer to the spiritual or immaterial part of a person. However, this would make one of these two words utterly redundant in Paul's prayer. So we are left with the only proper conclusion that spirit, soul and body are the three substantial parts of a human person. Paul literally writes (in the Greek) about 'the spirit and the soul and the body'. The arrangement of these three nouns with three definite articles connected by the word 'and' leads us to a single, natural explanation: that Paul sees the human person as a triunity of spirit, soul and body.

Human beings are made in the image of God, and God is triune. The Greek vision of humankind is replaced by a more Hebraic, trinitarian and holistic view.

What then is the difference between these three aspects of our humanity? The spirit is that part of our lives that is able to perceive and have communion with the spiritual realm. Until we are born again, our spirits are dead and can only relate to that which is dead in the spiritual (ie, the occult). When we are born again, our spirits become alive to God. The Holy Spirit infuses our human spirits, testifying that we are the adopted children of our heavenly Father (Romans 8:16). Through the atoning work of Jesus on the cross, our spirits (formerly dead) are now filled with the life of the age to come and empowered to have intimate communion with the Father. Only through the cross of Christ can the human spirit be rescued from its prison of darkness and death. As Charles Wesley put it:

> Long my imprisoned spirit lay
> Fast bound in sin and nature's night;
> Thine eye diffused a quickening ray –
> I woke, the dungeon flamed with light;
> My chains fell off, my heart was free.
> I rose, went forth, and followed thee.[7]

If the spirit is the part of our humanity that relates to the spiritual, the soul is the centre of our personality. Here the mental, emotional and volitional components that make up our unique identity are found. The soul is accordingly the *ego* or 'self', which in turn is made up of the mind, the emotions and the will. Through the physical body, the self relates to the world around it. Through the spirit, the self relates to the spiritual world (if regenerate, to the living God).

The benefits of the cross of Christ do not apply only to the spirit and (as God wills) to the physical body. They also apply to the soul. The human mind is the battlefield where Satan has sought since Eden to cause disintegration. Ever since the garden, Satan has been working to destroy the *shalom* or wholeness that the Father wants us to enjoy in our souls. Once he has succeeded in infecting the mind, then the emotions are also infected, and the human will is bent on a course of death rather than life. This work of infection is known in the New Testament as 'demonisation'. When Jesus began his ministry, he cast out demons everywhere he went. In fact, the predominant picture you have of Jesus in the Synoptic Gospels is of a divine exorcist, whose very presence causes power encounters with the demonic – encounters in which the demons always lose out.

Jesus came to set the captives free. He came to bring freedom as well as forgiveness. A substantial part of Jesus' work of liberation involves the ministry of deliverance. One of the great benefits of the finished work of the cross is deliverance from evil spirits. In this respect we should always remember that the cross is a triumph, not a tragedy. This is most clearly seen in John's Gospel. For a long time it troubled me that there are no deliverance miracles in this Gospel. Unlike the Synoptic Gospels (Matthew, Mark and Luke) we do not read of a single incident of Jesus casting out a demon. Nor do we find any summary statements making reference to Jesus' deliverance ministry in a particular area. Then, one day, it sank in. John knew the stories of Jesus' exorcisms because he knew the other Gospel traditions. The reason he chooses to omit them is that he wants to portray the cross as the great moment of deliverance. During the week before he died, Jesus said, 'Now the prince of this world will be driven out' (John 12:31). The verb 'drive out' is the same one that is used for casting out evil spirits in the Synoptic Gospels. We can draw only one conclusion from this: in the cosmic war between good and evil, the cross is not the place of defeat but the place of victory. As the Apostle Paul puts it in Colossians 2:15 – 'Having disarmed the powers and authorities, he made a public spectacle of them, triumphing over them by the cross.'

All this highlights the wonderful truth that we no longer need to be products of our past but products of the cross. As the Spirit applies the benefits of Calvary to our souls through deliverance ministry, God's power brings freedom from every wrong, toxic authority over our lives. This includes freedom from the curse of legalism. As Paul states:

> All who rely on observing the law are under a curse, for it is written: 'Cursed is everyone who does not continue to do everything written in the Book of the Law.' Clearly no-one is justified before God by the law, because, 'The righteous will live by faith.' The law is not based on faith; on the contrary, 'The man who does these things will live by them.' Christ redeemed us from the curse of the law by becoming a curse for us, for it is written: 'Cursed is everyone who is hung on a tree.'
>
> Galatians 3:10–13

There is absolutely no getting away from it: the cross is the place where Satan's power is destroyed. When we engage in deliverance ministry, we are engaging in a battle that has already been won! Minds can be set free. Emotions can be healed. The cross is therefore the sign of God's victory and the devil's defeat.

No story illustrates this more vividly for me than the one about the Emperor Constantine. On the eve of a great battle, facing superior numbers, Constantine prayed for help from the Christian God. The church father Eusebius records how Constantine that night received a vision of streams of light joining to form a cross. Above it was the inscription, *In hoc signo vinces*, 'In this sign you will conquer'. As Constantine pondered the meaning of this, Jesus appeared to him holding a cross, and told him to put this sign on his banner. His army was filled with courage and won a great victory.

Truly, the cross is the sign of triumph not disaster. In the deliverance ministry, the Spirit applies the victory of the cross to oppressed lives. As he does so, the enemy's hold is loosed and people are set free.

The whole gospel

Jesus saves! Jesus heals! Jesus delivers! Jesus brings salvation to our spirits, healing to our bodies, and deliverance to our souls. The work of the cross touches the three greatest areas of need that human beings have: forgiveness of sins, healing from sickness, and deliverance from bondage. It is for this reason that Jesus told his disciples to preach the gospel, heal the sick and cast out demons. The kingdom can only truly be advanced in the world through all three of these activities. As we engage in all three, the Holy Spirit applies the benefits of the finished work of the cross to people's lives. As a result, they find salvation (for their spirits), healing (for their bodies) and deliverance (for their souls).

All this points to the need for an integrated view of Christian mission. Our task is to keep together the words and the works, the message and the miracles, the proclamation and the demonstration. However, there is another respect in which Christian mission needs to be integrated.

Everything that I have written in this chapter really applies to the salvation, healing and deliverance of the individual. For some, whose passion is to see the church dealing with injustice, this will all feel far too individualistic. What about social justice, they will ask? What about the poor? What about the politically oppressed?

These are very important and justifiable questions. The mission statement of Jesus of Nazareth included preaching good news to the poor and the proclamation of freedom to prisoners. It involved release for the oppressed and the inauguration of a Jubilee. In short, Jesus introduced a social as well as a saving gospel.

None of this diminishes in any way the individual person's need for salvation. We cannot carry the love of God to the marginalised until we have ourselves received the fire of God's love. It is only as we receive the benefits of the cross through the work of the Spirit that we can then be of any lasting help to the helpless. It is only as we receive the power of God that we can be of any life-changing use to the powerless. There therefore has to be an initial focus on the individual's reception of all the blessings won at Calvary. Having said that, we are not supposed to turn personal salvation or personal revival into an end in itself. God's gifts are given to us so that we can give them away to others. Jesus sent the disciples out to preach, heal and deliver, because, as he goes on to say, 'Freely you have received, freely give' (Matthew 10:8). The disciples had been the recipients of grace themselves; as a result they were able to be good news to the lost sheep of Israel.

Like many believers, I have a hero of the Christian faith. He is a hero because he not only combined words and works (preaching the cross with demonstrations of the Spirit's power), he also managed to combine the social as well as the saving aspects of the Gospel. My great hero is

Norway's equivalent of John Wesley. His name is Hans Nielsen Hauge. Hauge lived from 1771 until 1824. He was brought up on a farm in the parish of Tune in the community of Rolfsoy. In fact, his surname Hauge was the name of the farm that his grandfather had acquired. As a thirteen-year-old, Hauge had a narrow escape when he nearly drowned while transporting a boatload of hay. This experience produced a high degree of soul-searching. Thereafter, Hauge spent his energies striving to be a devout, religious man.

The turning point in Hauge's life came on 5 April 1796. As he was ploughing his father's fields, he began to sing the Norwegian hymn, 'Jesus, I long for your blessed communion'. The words expressed his deep desire for internal reality rather than mere external religion. As he sang, the power of God overwhelmed him. Here is Hauge's own description of what happened next:

> My heart was so uplifted to God that I don't know nor can express what took place in my soul. As soon as my understanding returned, I regretted that I hadn't served the loving and all-gracious God; now I felt that no worldly thing was of any importance. It was a glory no tongue can explain; my soul felt something supernatural, divine and blessed. . . . I had a completely transformed mind, a sorrow over all sins, a burning desire that others should share the same grace, a particular desire to read the Scriptures, especially Jesus' own teachings, as well as new light to understand them.[8]

Having received his own salvation, Hauge now sought to spread the gospel throughout Norway. He distinctly heard the Lord saying, 'Whom shall I send out to carry the invitations to my great banquet?' Hauge replied, 'Send me.' Having freely and sovereignly received God's love, Hauge's heart now burned with love for his fellow men and women. As Hauge was later to write: 'When we are converted and receive God's love in our hearts, then we will love our neighbour, confess Jesus' name, and teach transgressors God's way so sinners can be converted.'[9]

For fourteen days Hauge hardly ate. Then he started to reach out to others, beginning in his own home. For the next eight years, Hauge made eight evangelistic journeys, covering some ten thousand miles of Norwegian soil on ski and on foot. Thousands entered salvation as Hauge preached the gospel, and there were demonstrations of the Spirit's power. Indeed, Hauge's followers were often accused of unattractive mannerisms and fanatical behaviour. These were due to the physical and emotional responses they showed to the empowering presence of God which attended Hauge's preaching of the gospel.

Hauge's impact was, however, far greater than on individuals alone. He also influenced the whole nation socially and politically, and in ways that even secular historians acknowledge were beneficial. Here are some examples of the ways in which Hauge and his followers brought social changes:

1. Hauge broke with the unwritten law that a peasant should stay in the place where he was born and raised, and that each person should remain in his calling. He thereby brought liberation to others like himself.
2. His example encouraged people to enter industries that they had not been born into.
3. He spoke and wrote in a language that ordinary people could understand, thereby making the gospel far more accessible to the poor than it had been.
4. He wrote thirty-three books in all, mostly between 1796 and 1804. These promoted literacy among the peasant classes and helped ordinary people to relate

their faith to daily life.

5. His books resulted in the paper and printing industries being developed in Norway. Hauge also introduced recycling to Norway in his paper mills.

6. As a young man himself (in his twenties), Hauge used and released young people in his itinerant ministry and his printing presses.

7. He allowed women to preach, thereby releasing them to make a vital impact in a male-dominated arena.

8. His ministry also gave licence for lay people (not just ordained state church pastors) to preach.

9. His ministry brought an end to alcoholism, gambling, swearing and other vices in many districts.

10. He knitted jumpers and mittens as he walked and then gave them to the poor.

11. Before he preached to people in a community, he would share the latest ideas about farming practices and equipment. He also helped on the farms himself. He helped to raise agricultural standards right across the nation.

12. He helped set up small industries in places where his message was readily accepted.

13. He was the first person to employ disabled people in his factory, thereby sowing the seeds of the principle of equal opportunities.

14. In 1809, when salt was in short supply, Hauge was released from prison for eight months. He found out where the salt around the coastal waters was richest and set up salt factories on the west and south coasts of Norway. During times of famine, Hauge and his followers ensured that the hungry were fed.

15. He encouraged farmers in the south of Norway to areas around Trondheim in the north of Norway. These poorer areas were subsequently greatly and lastingly

improved both economically and spiritually.

Hauge is impressive because he managed to combine the saving and the social implications of the gospel in an extremely creative way. Hauge empowered people to express themselves socially. In short, he gave a voice to those without a voice.

However, it was this that eventually led him into trouble. As a direct result of Hauge's work, a strong unity was beginning to emerge among the lower classes in Norway. A nationwide network of people was established and sustained through Hauge's letters, and this caused considerable anxiety at a time when the French Revolution was still fresh in people's minds. The state authorities therefore became very nervous. Those who were infected by the rationalism of the Enlightenment were intimidated because they felt that social change should come from the top down, not from the bottom up. So Hauge was arrested and imprisoned in 1804, when he was only thirty-three years old, and not released until 1814. The suffering of his time in prison took its toll and Hauge died a few years later, in 1821.

We could all learn from Hauge. In his life we see the Spirit applying the benefits of the cross not just to individuals but to communities, and not just to communities but to an entire nation. Salvation for Hauge was not allowed to become a privatised experience. Rather, as the Holy Spirit applied the Calvary love of God to Hauge, Hauge in turn sought to give that same love away to others.

As we consider the work of the cross and the work of the Spirit in relation to 'mission', we need to recapture a vision for the whole gospel. The work of the cross is to be applied to the whole person (not just the spiritual) and to the whole of society (not just the individual). Though there is not much to suggest a ministry of healing and deliverance in his life, Hans Nielsen Hauge's example is a compelling and challenging one in this regard. Would that God would raise up a generation of Hauges today, in Scandinavia, in Europe, in the world. As the prophet Habakkuk prayed:

> LORD, I have heard of your fame;
> I stand in awe of your deeds, O LORD.
> Renew them in our day,
> in our time make them known;
> in wrath remember mercy.

Habakkuk 3:2

Chapter 6

BRILLIANCE AND BROKENNESS

*I want to know Christ and the power of his resurrection and
the fellowship of sharing in his sufferings, becoming like
him in his death, and so, somehow, to attain to the
resurrection from the dead.*

Philippians 3:10–11

*Every Christian knows, through personal experience, that
the Christian life is lived on two tracks, power and pain. . . .
Our belief in the power of God always runs side-by-side
with our experience of pain and suffering.*

Rich Nathan and Ken Wilson, *Empowered Evangelicals.
Bringing Together the Best of the Evangelical and
Charismatic Worlds*[1]

At the end of the last chapter I wrote about Hans Nielsen
Hauge, who was used by God to bring revival to Norway
during the era of the Napoleonic wars. Hauge was a man
filled with the fire of God, who preached the gospel with

demonstrations of the Spirit's power. But he was also a man who experienced considerable suffering. He was arrested a number of times before finally being imprisoned for ten years. For Hauge, following Christ was not just a matter of preaching in the revival power of the Holy Spirit. It also involved participating in the sufferings of Christ.

One of the most poignant stories about Hauge dates from the first year of his long imprisonment (1804-1805). Hauge's supporters were tempted to fall into despair. The future looked bleak and the situation looked very dark for the revival generally.

In December 1804, Hauge was in prison in Oslo during a wet, cold and miserable winter. Hauge spent his time sitting at his high prison window, looking at the snow-covered streets, watching the passers-by. A lone figure went by, then paused, then turned back towards the façade of the prison building. Hauge realised what was going on. A friend had clearly come to see him but had been denied entrance. This man was now surveying the windows of the upper storey of the prison.

Hauge recognised the man immediately as a friend from the west coast of Norway. His clothes gave him away. He was probably from around Bergen. He had travelled for a very long time, some of the way on foot and on skis. Now it looked as though all his efforts had been wasted and that he would have to return the way he came.

Hauge grabbed hold of the candle and held it up to the window of his cell. His friend saw it, stopped still, and watched. As the flame flickered, the friend saw a hand appear to trim the wick so that the light could shine even brighter. Immediately the friend understood the signal and started his journey home across the mountains, this time with a glad rather than a sad heart. Everywhere he went he spread the same message to Hauge's followers, 'that the light which is to shine before men must be cleansed of all unworthy motives. The purified light burns brightest and sends its blessed rays far out into the night.'[2]

Cracked pots

In 2 Corinthians 4, the Apostle Paul talks about the strange paradox of brokenness and brilliance. On the one hand there is brokenness in the Christian life. As believers, we are like fragile jars of clay. We are not priceless Grecian urns. We are ordinary clay pots whose trials and tribulations have produced fissures and holes. Indeed, we are in a real sense cracked pots. We are broken and we are made from the earth.

On the other hand, it is the very fact of our brokenness that results in our brilliance. Put a lit candle in a perfect pot and it will quickly be extinguished through lack of oxygen. Put it in a cracked pot and the light will continue to shine because air is coming through the gaps. Indeed, the more broken we are, the more brilliant the light will be. The more cracks there are, the less the pot will be able to keep the light to itself. Indeed, it is the very presence of these cracks that leads to the refraction of the light of the glory of Christ for others. So while we experience in this life the fellowship of the cross, we also shine with the all-surpassing power of God.

Not long ago a friend of mine had a dream.[3] He saw a man with an expensively wrapped present, the size of a shoe box. He was giving this gift to another man, who was clearly a brother or a friend. The second man opened up the gift with great excitement, unwrapping a beautiful set of cups. They were antiques, hand-painted, and of great value. The only problem was that every single one had a crack in it so it was obvious they could not be used to hold liquid.

The man said, 'Thank you', because he did not want to appear ungrateful and then left with his gift. Having returned home he did not know what to do with the cups. In the end he decided to put them all on a shelf in his attic.

At this moment the dream sequence changed. The scene now shifted to heaven. Someone had brought one of the cups to the Lord Jesus. Jesus held the cup in his hands as if it were of immense value. The man heard Jesus say, 'Do you know why this cup is valuable to me?' 'No,' replied the man. Jesus continued, 'This cup is so precious because I can pour my glory into it and it won't keep it for itself.'

In this final chapter, we examine the various ways in which the light of the Spirit pours out of a life lived in fellowship with the cross. We explore the paradox of power in weakness. We will see how the Holy Spirit brings us into fellowship with the cross in water baptism, in discipleship, in our constant battle against sin, in seasons of surrender and consecration, and in times of hardship and in death. In all of these ways, the Holy Spirit works with us in our brokenness so that the brilliant light of his glory can shine in and through our lives.

Baptism in water

Our study begins with an investigation of water baptism. On the day of Pentecost, Peter exhorted his listeners as follows:

> Repent and *be baptised*, every one of you, in the name of Jesus Christ so that your sins may be forgiven. And you will receive the gift of the Holy Spirit. The promise is for you and your children and for all who are far off – for all whom the Lord our God will call.
>
> Acts 2:38–39, my italics

That day, three thousand people responded. They were baptised in the *mikveh* pools just outside the Temple building. These pools, and there were many of them, were supposed to be used for ritual washing prior to entering the Temple. Now they were used for baptising new believers in Jesus. It must have been an extraordinary sight!

What connection does baptism have with the Spirit and the cross? In baptism the Holy Spirit formally seals a person's fellowship in the cross. Just as Jesus died and was buried, so we acknowledge at our baptism that we are now dead to sin and that the old ego-centred life is over. Water baptism is therefore a kind of funeral. The good news is that there is an immediate resurrection!

Baptism is an outward sign of our identification with the cross and resurrection of Christ. As we go under the water it is like drowning. As we are lifted up from the water and breathe air into our lungs it is like living again. Baptism in water is accordingly a public act in which we signify that we have died to sin and are now living in the new life of the Spirit. More than that, it is an act in which we are plunged into the death and resurrection of Jesus Christ. As Paul puts it:

> Don't you know that all of us who were baptised into Christ Jesus were baptised into his death? We were therefore buried with him through baptism into death in order that, just as Christ was raised from the dead through the glory of the Father, we too may live a new life.
>
> Romans 6:3–4

In our water baptism, the Holy Spirit unites us to Jesus Christ in his death at Calvary. As we are immersed in the baptismal waters (by those performing the baptism), the grace of God is at work in our lives in the person and power of the Holy Spirit. The Spirit applies the work of the cross to our lives as we formally and publicly say a resounding 'NO' to the life of the flesh. As we do so, the benefits of Calvary are once again actualised as we are washed in the waters.

But baptism does not end with us under the waters. If it did, we would be literally dead as opposed to dead to sin! As we say a resounding 'YES' to the new life that Jesus offers, the Spirit applies the work of the resurrection to our lives. In other words, that same life-giving power that raised the Son of God fills our mortal bodies afresh. This is why there is sometimes an actual manifestation of the Spirit's power in the bodies of the newly baptised. On occasions I have seen people having to be carried out of a baptismal pool because they are so overcome by the power of the Spirit. Not only has the Spirit applied the work of the cross to their lives. He has also applied the awesome, mighty work of the resurrection.

Water baptism is accordingly an outward, public sign of the fact that we have been crucified and raised with Jesus Christ through the power of the Holy Spirit.

The cross and the crown

From baptism onwards, the Christian life involves a growing fellowship in the work of the cross and the work of the Spirit. True Christian discipleship is an *imitatio Christi*, an imitation of Christ. In the life of Jesus the Messiah we see the work of the Spirit and the work of the cross in an integrated relationship. This is very evident in Mark's Gospel where the story as a whole is divided into two equal halves, the first stressing miracles (Mark 1:13 – 8:30), the second stressing martyrdom (Mark 8:31 – 15:47).[4]

In the first half of Mark's Gospel, Jesus performs many

signs and wonders. These events can be grouped into healing, exorcism, nature and resurrection miracles. The healing miracles can be found in 1:29, 40; 2:1; 3:1, 7; 5:21; 6:1,
53; 7:31 and 8.22. The exorcism miracles are at 1:21,34b; 5:1
and 7:24. The nature miracles are at 4:35; 6:30, 45 and 8:1.
The only resurrection miracle (Jairus' daughter) is at 5:35ff.
During the first half of Mark's Gospel, the focus is very
much on Jesus' power and authority, both of which derive
from the work of the Holy Spirit in his life.

If we only had Mark 1:13 – 8:30, we would have a *theologia gloriae*, a theology of glory. However, the picture
changes dramatically after Peter's confession of Christ at
Caesarea Philippi. From Mark 8:31 onwards, the focus is
not so much on miracles as on martyrdom, not so much on
a *theologia gloriae* as a *theologia crucis* (a theology of the
cross). Indeed, there are only three more miracles in the
ministry of Jesus after 8:31 (9:14–29; 10:46–52 and
11:12–14,20–21). The change of emphasis is registered right
at the beginning of the second half of Mark's Gospel as
Jesus makes the first of three predictions of his passion at
8:31 (see also 9:31 and 10:33): 'He then began to teach them
that the Son of Man must suffer many things and be rejected by the elders, chief priests and teachers of the law, and
that he must be killed and after three days rise again.'

Peter, of course, complains. He can easily follow a man
of the Spirit, not so easily a man of the cross. Jesus repri-
mands Peter by telling him that the way of discipleship
must involve the work of the cross as well as the work of
the Spirit. As the master shall the servant be: 'If anyone
would come after me, he must deny himself and take up
his cross and follow me. For whoever wants to save his life
will lose it, but whoever loses his life for me and for the
gospel will save it (Mark 8:34b–35).'

We cannot avoid the implications of this very simple

structure. Mark wants his readers to understand that the way of discipleship involves suffering as well as glory, martyrdom as well as miracles, the cross as well as the Spirit. This integrated vision of discipleship is beautifully captured in the story of the healing of blind Bartimaeus in Mark 10:46–52. At the start of the story, Mark writes that Bartimaeus was sitting by the roadside begging. In the Greek, the word translated 'road' also means 'way' (*hodos*). What we see therefore is a man called Bartimaeus sitting 'by the way'.

Bartimaeus hears that Jesus is coming and shouts persistently for mercy. Jesus stops and asks the disciples to call the blind man. Bartimaeus throws his cloak aside and comes to Jesus. He explains that he wants to see, and Jesus performs a miracle. Jesus tells the man to go, but instead he follows Jesus 'on the way' (*hodos*).

If ever there was a Gospel account that harmonised wonders and weakness it is this. Bartimaeus clearly receives a miracle in this story. Once he was blind, but now he can see. In short, he experiences the work of the Spirit in his life. At the same time, he embarks on a life of costly discipleship. Having begun by sitting by the way, he ends by being on the way. Where is this way leading? To Jerusalem, to Calvary, to the cross of Christ (Mark 10:32). The first Christians were called 'followers of the *hodos* or way' (Acts 9:2; 19:9, 23; 22:4; 24:14, 22). The 'way' is the way of the Messiah Jesus. This reveals something very interesting about Bartimaeus: not only does he embrace the work of the Spirit; he also embraces the work of the cross.

The way of discipleship is therefore a lifelong process of sharing in the fellowship of Christ's sufferings and walking in the supernatural power of God. It is not a case of *either* the cross *or* the Spirit. It is both the cross *and* the Spirit. The road of shallow triumphalism and constant success is not the way of discipleship at all. But neither is the road of joyless piety and incessant defeat. There are undoubtedly some charismatic Christians who indulge in an almost cross-less form of discipleship (what Dietrich Bonhoeffer called 'cheap' as opposed to 'costly' grace[5]). But there are equally many Christians who have embraced an almost Spirit-less form of discipleship in which there is no experience of God's power and no expectation of the miraculous. Neither of these represents a comprehensive, biblical vision of discipleship. We must give our heavenly Father complete freedom to apply both the work of the cross and the work of the Spirit in our lives. We must be open to suffering as well as glory.

A daily crucifixion

In our baptism and discipleship, the work of the Spirit and the work of the cross are united. In both our beginning and our continuing, we have fellowship in the cross through the power of God's Spirit.

But within this lifelong journey there are other ways in which the Spirit and the cross are united. Here we must at long last deal with the subject of sanctification. The word 'sanctification' means the process by which we are made holy. Holy means 'set apart from the world's values and behaviour'. It also means 'pure' and 'clean' in our thoughts as well as our words and actions. Sanctification is therefore a process of progressive transformation in which we become increasingly clean on the inside. It is the journey towards moral perfection. Sanctification begins at our *conversion* and ends at the *completion* of our Christian lives. Between these two events, there is the task of co-operating with the Holy Spirit so that we can become increasingly holy in the *continuation* of our Christian walk.

Just as there are some Christians who stress the cross and others who stress the Spirit, so there are some who say that sanctification is an active process and others who say that it is passive. In other words, some argue that we become holy through our own self-discipline and effort, as we fight the good fight against the world, the flesh and the devil. Others, on the other hand, argue that we become holy as we allow the Holy Spirit (the Spirit of holiness) to fill our lives more and more, with the inevitable consequence that we become more like Jesus. The first group focuses on the cross and suggests that holiness is all up to us. The second focuses on the Spirit and suggests that it is all up to God.

In reality, we become holy by both giving and receiving. We give ourselves to the task of crucifying our flesh. But in the process we receive the help of the Holy Spirit. On the one hand, then, we have to play our part actively. Thomas à Kempis outlines the role we play. He exhorts us

> to resist the appetites of the body and bring them in absolute subjection to the Spirit; to shun honours; to receive affronts with meekness; to be content to be despised by others; to bear with calm resignation the loss of fortune, health and friends; to have no desire after the riches, the honours and the pleasures of the world.

On the other hand, we need the help of the Holy Spirit because there is no power inherent within our humanity with which we can do such things. So à Kempis continues:

> If you depend upon your own will and strength to do and suffer all this, you will find yourself as unable to accomplish it as to create another world. But if you turn to the divine power within yourself, and trust only to that as the doer and sufferer

of all, the strength of omnipotence will be imparted to you, and the world and the flesh will be put under your feet.[6]

It is here that we need to dwell briefly on the much neglected topic of mortification. Mortification is simply dying to sin. To mortify the flesh, with all its sinful desires, is to crucify it. Note here the finality of the imagery. Mortification is not a temporary abstinence from sin. It is a brutal execution and termination of it.

The passage in the New Testament that gives the clearest teaching on this subject is Romans 8:13–14. Here the Apostle Paul writes: 'If you live according to the sinful nature, you will die; but if by the Spirit you put to death the misdeeds of the body, you will live, because those who are led by the Spirit of God are sons of God.'

In this very compact statement, Paul speaks about 'mortification'. The verb is in the present continuous, so Paul is talking about a lifelong process of crucifixion, not just a one-off event. Furthermore, the believer is the subject of this verb. This shows that we ourselves need to be active in the crucifixion of the flesh. Paul says, 'YOU put it to death.' No one else is going to do this for us. Furthermore, Paul mentions what it is we have to crucify – 'the misdeeds of the body.' In Colossians 3 Paul spells out what some of these 'misdeeds' are: 'sexual immorality, impurity, lust, evil desires and greed, which is idolatry'(v.5), and 'anger, rage, malice, slander and filthy language'(v.8).

Thankfully, we do not have to terminate all these vices in our own strength alone. We do not have to go the extremes that were evident in the Middle Ages and beat our bodies physically into submission. The good news in Romans 8:13–14 is that we put the flesh to death 'by the Spirit'. The word here is *pneumati*, which refers to the Spirit of God and not the human spirit of men and women. Furthermore, *pneumati* is what is called an instrumental dative, which shows that we have the Spirit's help in the work of mortification. God's Spirit helps us in the daily process of dying to self. Mortification is therefore like treating cancer. We target the cancerous tissue that needs to be destroyed. God directs the laser beam of his Spirit on the cancer as we focus all our efforts on obliterating its presence in our flesh.

The work of mortification is therefore another way in which the Holy Spirit leads us into a deeper fellowship with the cross in our lives. No one ever became holy by mere self-effort, so it is reassuring to hear that we have the Holy Spirit to help us. But no one ever received a perfect Christian character through the laying on of hands. So it is challenging to hear that we have to fight the battle ourselves.

Someone has said that many Christians today are much better at falling in the Spirit than walking in the Spirit. One of the reasons for this is that we have presented the cross in a one-sided way. We have spoken of the atoning work of the cross as an objective truth. But we have not taught about the refining work of the cross as a subjective reality. Put another way, we have spoken about the *fact* of the cross but not about its *fellowship*. This has led to believers' resting in the pardon they have received, but then failing to live a life in imitation of the crucified Messiah.

The neglect of this teaching on mortification has done considerable harm to the body of Christ and has produced a generation of consumeristic believers who want the life of the Spirit without the crucifixion of their flesh. Paul, however, is adamant. There must be a continuous application of the work of the cross to our flesh if we are to live in the fullness of God's power. The cross leads to the Spirit. As Father Michael Duggan has put it:

Continual daily repentance, understood as a practical handing over of the drives of the self life to the power of the cross and a turning to the grace that is ours in the Holy Spirit, will always bring us to experience more deeply the vast wealth of life that is ours through baptism in the Holy Spirit.[7]

Seasons of surrender

As we continue on the road of sanctification, there are, I believe, special times when our Father in heaven calls us to greater levels of abandonment. I call these seasons of surrender. They are periods of our Christian lives when the Holy Spirit takes us to the cross, not so much to deal with specific sins that need to die, but to deal with the tendency we have to depend upon ourselves rather than on God. At these times, God's intention is to deal with the issue of sin rather than sins. Sin (singular) is our tendency to manage on our own, to depend upon our own strength, and to follow our own desires. Sins (plural) are acts that spring from this fundamental attitude of independence. Seasons of surrender are times when we are brought to a place of complete weakness, when we come to the very end of our own human resources, and when we abandon ourselves completely to the Father's will and the Father's ways. The result of these times is a release of great spiritual power in our lives. As we surrender all at the cross, the Father pours out his Spirit and we experience new life and power.

It seems to me that the Apostle Paul experienced a number of these seasons. He refers to the matter of weakness a great deal in his letters. In fact, more than half of the nearly 50 references to weakness in the New Testament occur in 1 and 2 Corinthians! The great theme of 2 Corinthians is the divine power that comes out of human weakness. The prime example is 2 Corinthians 12:9. Having prayed three times for the removal of his mysterious thorn in the flesh, Paul hears the Holy Spirit saying to him, 'My grace is sufficient for you, for my power is made perfect in weakness.'

Why is it that the Father would want a man like Paul to experience weakness? The answer is simple. Because Paul had so many strengths! He was obviously extraordinarily clever, extremely well educated, and socially well privileged. While these strengths were a great asset in his defence of the gospel, they could also be a great obstacle to his total dependence upon God. So the Father allowed Paul to experience seasons in which he came to the end of himself, which of course is the beginning of God. God allowed Paul to experience what I call the Zerubbabel syndrome – the revelation that it is not by human might nor by human strength but by God's Spirit that mountain difficulties are levelled (Zechariah 4:6). These times were no doubt painful for Paul, but they were also the path to greater power.

There are therefore seasons of surrender for all of us in our Christian lives. At these times we are confronted by our weakness. The reason we are brought so low is in order that we might have breakthroughs, not breakdowns. Jesus was crucified in weakness, yet lives by God's power. And we are brought to a place of weakness, so that the power of Christ may rest upon us in a new and dynamic way (2 Corinthians 12:9; 13:4). As we embrace the death process in which our self-confidence and self-reliance are crucified, so the anointing comes for triumphs we thought were impossible. It is all so reminiscent of Gideon, who witnessed God stripping away almost his entire army, before empowering him to sound the trumpet and win a great victory against all the odds. Most, if not all of us, will experience such seasons when all is stripped away, especially if we are called to spiritual leadership. These times of vulnerability are not to be rebuked, as if they were something evil. They should be seen for what they are – the divine path to victory.

So we read throughout church history of how seasons of revival are preceded by times of personal surrender. In situations where the church seemed to be dying on its feet, God sought out individuals who were prepared to surrender everything and consecrate themselves to him in radical ways. Men like John Wesley were brought to an intense awareness of their weaknesses, before God empowered them to bring life to a dying nation. The same was true of Evan Roberts, Douglas Brown and Duncan Campbell – the revivalists of the twentieth century in Britain.[8] Before God did a great work through these people, he had to do a great work in them. It was as if he said to them what he had said to the people in Joshua's time: 'Consecrate yourselves, for tomorrow [I] will do amazing things among you' (Joshua 3:1–5).

So here we find another way in which the Holy Spirit brings us into the fellowship of the cross. These are seasons in which our human nature is crucified as we willingly surrender all to God. These are seasons when our prayer is:

> All to Jesus, I surrender,
> Lord, I give myself to Thee;
> Fill me with thy love and power,
> Let thy blessing fall on me.[9]

We cannot have the power of the Spirit without a prior death to self, to striving, to success, and the like. As Andrew Murray put it: 'In the likeness and weakness and death which we shall taste in the fellowship of the crucified, a secret door will be opened into the place of God's power which all our willing and running could never discover.[10]

Difficulties and opportunities

It should by now be evident that one of the great ministries of the Holy Spirit has to do with 'identification'. The Spirit enables us to identify with Jesus Christ in his death and resurrection. One of the tasks of the Spirit is therefore to make real in our actual experience the truth that we have been crucified with Christ (Galatians 2:20). As an objective fact, we are dead to sin. On the cross, everything that caused us to sin (the world, the flesh and the devil) has been disarmed. Everything that had authority over our lives and caused us to sin has been defeated. When Jesus went to the cross, he not only took our sin, he took us too! Subjectively, however, we need to live as people who have died. With the help of the Spirit, we need constantly to crucify the misdeeds of our bodies and to put our self-life to death.

On Death Row in certain American states, a condemned prisoner will be heralded with words of respect, 'Dead man walking'. The same thing should be said of followers of Christ. We are dead men walking. We were dead *in* sin before we were born again. Now we are dead *to* sin. Our part each day is actually to *believe* this truth. Every time we see something that we find tempting and seductive, we need to declare, 'No, I have died to that.' Every time we are tempted to say something that grieves the Holy Spirit, we need to say, 'That kind of talk is dead in my life.' Every time we sense something in our hearts that is clearly contrary to the word of God we need to say, 'That has been put to death already.' In other words, we need to believe and behave as people who live under one authority, the Lordship of Christ. Every other false and toxic authority has been destroyed through the work of the cross.

This is why Paul could speak about carrying around in one's body the death of Jesus so that the life of Jesus may also be revealed (2 Corinthians 4:10). Paul is talking again about the way in which the Holy Spirit brings us into fellowship with the cross. However, it should be noted that the means by which this fellowship can happen actually vary. So far we have been talking about baptism, discipleship, mortification and surrender as the means. However, there are other ways too. The immediate context of 2 Corinthians 4:10 concerns hardship. In vv. 8–9, Paul has this to say: 'We are hard pressed on every side, but not crushed; perplexed, but not in despair; persecuted, but not abandoned; struck down, but not destroyed.' Evidently Paul felt that the Holy Spirit could use any trial as the means by which we could carry in our bodies the death of Jesus.

A man I know called Bill went to a special healing service at a local charismatic church. Although he was a member of this church, he was very sceptical about the Holy Spirit and especially about experiencing anything. He regarded all this as shallow emotionalism.

Bill's life was full of hardship. His wife June was suffering from advanced Alzheimer's disease and was in full-time residential care. Whenever Bill went to visit her, she did not recognise him. His visits were becoming more and more difficult, and he found himself losing a sense of his love for her. The times on Saturday afternoon in the nursing home had become a desperate ordeal as he sat unrecognised by the woman he had loved with all his heart for over forty years. All this pain, on top of his scepticism about things 'charismatic', did not put Bill in a particularly positive frame of mind as the healing meeting started that evening.

After a time of worship, the visiting speaker stood up and talked from Scripture and his own experience about the power of God. At the end, the speaker asked people to come forward for ministry. Again, without being conscious of exactly how he got there, Bill found himself at the front of the church receiving prayer. To his amazement, he experienced the power of God come upon him, and he fell to the floor.

Over the next few minutes, as he lay there, he began to feel the wounds of Jesus in his hands and feet. After the meeting, he walked home and went to bed. During the night, the pain from these wounds got worse. In the morning Bill asked the Lord to explain the significance of what he was experiencing. He sensed that the Holy Spirit was revealing just how much Jesus identified with his suffering, and indeed June's.

That afternoon, Bill went back to the nursing home with a renewed sense of love for his wife. For the first time in a long while she actually recognised him and they spent all afternoon kissing and cuddling. Bill was there for hours. Indeed, the same thing happened the following Saturday! Although June subsequently relapsed, Bill feels that the Lord wanted them to have that precious time together. He felt comforted that the Lord knew exactly how they felt, that he was with them in their suffering, and that everything was part of his sovereign purpose.

Here is an example of the way in which the Holy Spirit can use hardships to bring us into closer fellowship with the cross. An appalling difficulty became an opportunity in the hands of the Holy Spirit. In the awful situation in which Bill and June found themselves, they experienced the ministry of the comforter in their identification with the cross of Christ.

The art of dying

Not only does the Spirit give us fellowship with the cross during the course of our lives, he also does the same at the end of our lives. I am talking now about our dying and our death. For a Christian, the moment of death is a moment of abandonment. 'Father, into your hands I commit my spirit.' Empowered by the Spirit, we face death with the same dignity, love and radiance that Jesus of Nazareth did. The same Holy Spirit that enabled him to endure his sufferings is at work in us as well. Just as Calvary was the doorway to the resurrection for Jesus, so it is for the Christian believer. The cross leads to the Spirit in death as in life.

I have seen quite a number of people prepare for death, but I have never seen the radiance of the Holy Spirit as I have in George Knight. George was a much loved member of St Andrew's, and known affectionately as Grandpa George. He was diagnosed with lung cancer and, in spite of much prayer, he deteriorated. In the last week of his life I visited him in hospital. I asked him how he was physically, and – between short breaths – he told me with a smile on his face that he was dying. I asked him how he was spiritually, and he replied with one word, 'wonderful'.

George's three sons – Steve, Chris and Mark, all of them committed Christians, like their dad – had started preparing a room for George to die in at home. They were redecorating it for their dad's last few days. But George looked at me with a twinkle in his eye and said, 'I'm not going there. There is a room already prepared for me in my Father's house.' George's face lit up as he spoke.

A few days later George died. Hundreds of us gathered at St Andrew's to give thanks to the Lord. I can safely say that I have never been at a funeral like it – so full of love, joy, laughter, hope and the powerful presence of the Holy Spirit. Non-Christians were profoundly touched. One neighbour of George's, for whom he had been praying over many years, was heard to say, 'I am going to have to become a Christian now, otherwise I will never see George again.'

What is it that George had in his life as he walked to the end of his Calvary road? He had the life of the age to come in his mortal body. While his body was dying, his spirit was alive with the power of the resurrection. As George shared in the fellowship of Christ's sufferings in the final weeks of his life, he also knew the power of the resurrection. So while he became like Jesus in his death, we also knew he had attained the resurrection from the dead (Philippians 3:10–11).

All this highlights the way in which the work of the Spirit and the work of the cross continue right up to the very end of our lives. In fact, we are no less Spirit-filled in our dying than we are in our living. Jesus did not cease being charismatic as he approached his death. Nor do we.

A fine example of this is given in Jonathan Edwards' account of the great revival in Northampton, USA in 1736. He describes the life and death of a certain young woman called Abigail Hutchinson.[11] 'She was of an intelligent family,' Edwards writes, and 'there could be nothing in her education that tended to enthusiasm, but rather to the contrary extreme.' It was not Abigail's tendency to be 'ostentatious of experiences'; she was 'still, quiet and reserved'.

She had been ill for quite a while by the time the revival broke out. For three days she was in great distress concerning her sinfulness; 'she wondered and was astonished at herself, that she had been so concerned for her body, and had applied so often to physicians to heal that, and had neglected her soul.' At the end of it, however, she had a vision of Jesus Christ and the assurance that the blood of Christ had cleansed her from all sin. From that time on, 'there was a constant sweetness in her soul'.

Edwards describes the extraordinary fruit of this conversion. He notes that Abigail had a 'distress for Christless persons' and that 'she felt a strong inclination immediately to go forth to warn sinners'. She developed an intense love for everyone. She was often overcome in the presence of other godly people. She 'had many extraordinary discoveries of the glory of God and Christ', meditating on God's eternal attributes and often seeing visions of Calvary. While reading the Bible, she would often experience 'the powerful breathings of the Spirit of God on her soul'. Most of all, she had 'great longings to die, so that she might be with Christ'. She was heard to say: 'I am quite willing to live, and quite willing to die; quite willing to be sick, and quite willing to be well; and quite willing for anything that God will bring upon me.' From that point on, Edwards writes, she felt herself in perfect submission to the will of God.

After this, her illness increased. Once, after spending the greater part of the night in extreme pain, she said, 'I am willing to suffer for Christ's sake; I am willing to spend and be spent for Christ's sake; I am willing to spend my life, even my very life, for Christ's sake!'

Abigail was suffering from a cancer that was causing a blockage in her throat yet she remained radiant until the end. People who saw her were greatly moved to see how she bore her sufferings, 'and were filled with admiration at her unexampled patience'. She often said to her sister, under extreme suffering, 'It is good to be so'. As she lay on her death-bed, she would say the words, 'God is my friend!' And on one occasion she turned to her sister and said, 'How sweet and comfortable it is to consider, and think of, heavenly things!'

It was some considerable time before Abigail died. Just prior to her death, she was asked whether she feared dying. She answered: 'There is indeed a dark entry, that looks something dark, but on the other side there appears such a bright shining light, that I cannot be afraid!'

Abigail Hutchison died 'as a person that went to sleep, without any struggling, about noon, on Friday June 27, 1735'. Edwards, reflecting on her life, admits with great integrity that some of her visionary experiences may have been due to the frailty of her condition. But he also acknowledges the extraordinary longing for heaven which she had, and he reports that 'she was looked upon amongst us as a very eminent instance of Christian experience'. Indeed, Edwards uses her story to give the reader a clearer idea of 'the nature and manner of the operation of God's Spirit, in this wonderful effusion' during the Great Awakening. Out of all the many stories of great works of power during the revival, Jonathan Edwards singles out a woman who exemplified 'the art of dying' as the most shining example. The Spirit gives us fellowship with the cross in our dying as well as our living.

Martyrdom and miracles

Perhaps nowhere is a believer's fellowship in the cross more evident than in martyrdom. The death of the first martyr, Stephen, is a case in point. We know the facts – how Stephen was a man filled with the grace of God, how he performed many miracles, how his face shone like an angel, how he was arrested, tried and sentenced to death. Even in his trial, Stephen continued to be filled with the Spirit, uttering words of wisdom that no one could refute. At his death Stephen was full of the Holy Spirit and had a vision of Jesus standing at the right hand of God. As many others have pointed out, this is the one time the ascended Jesus is seen standing rather than seated at the throne of heaven, giving an ovation, perhaps, for Stephen's faithfulness.

In his last moments, Stephen conducts himself in a way that is very reminiscent of Calvary. Like Jesus, Stephen prays that the Lord will receive his spirit. Like Jesus, Stephen forgives those who are executing him, praying, 'Lord, do not hold this sin against them' (Acts 7:60). It seems at a number of points as if the Spirit is applying the cross to Stephen in a literal way.

Truly, martyrdom and miracles are woven together in Stephen's final moments on earth. Notice, too, the fruit from this death. Jesus said, 'I tell you the truth, unless an ear of wheat falls to the ground and dies, it remains only a single seed. But if it dies, it produces many seeds. The man who loves his life will lose it, while the man who hates his life in this world will keep it for eternal life' (John 12:24–25). Stephen's example in death brings lasting fruit in the conversion of Saul of Tarsus, who witnesses the whole event. Death for Stephen means life for Paul. As we have seen so often in this book, the cross leads to the Spirit.

God's power is therefore present in our pain, especially in the case of martyrdom. James Bradley's essay on 'Miracles and Martyrdom in the Early Church' is instructive here.[12] Bradley's argument is that the early church had an integrated vision that combined vulnerability and victory.

Bradley first of all proves that the early church continues to witness miracles after the end of the first century. He defines the 'miraculous' as a broad category including gifts of utterance (such as prophecy) as well as healing, exorcism and even raising the dead. He quotes Bishop Irenaeus (from AD 180):

Some have foreknowledge of things to come: they see visions and utter prophetic expressions. Others still heal the sick by laying their hands upon them, and they are made whole. Yea, moreover, as I have said, the dead even have been raised up, and remained among us for many years.

Against Heresies, 2.32.4

Bradley concludes that the most prominent church leaders in Asia Minor, southern Gaul, North Africa, Egypt and Rome all bear witness to the fact that miracles were part and parcel of the Christian life.

Bradley also goes on to show that works of the Spirit's power were mainly talked about in connection with martyrdom. Justin Martyr refers to miracles done in the name of Jesus Christ 'who was crucified under Pontius Pilate', as does Irenaeus. Here the source of the Spirit's power is clearly attributed to the cross. Furthermore, references to miracles often occur in passages to do with persecution. He finds passages in Tertullian and Cyprian which show how visions were given as a means of comfort to those about to die as Christians.

A particularly vivid example of this (not quoted by Bradley) is the martyrdom of Saturus. Before he, Perpetua and Felicity are martyred in the arena at Carthage (in AD 203), Saturus has the following vision:

Our martyrdom was over. We had left our bodies behind. Four angels carried us towards the East but their hands did not touch us. . . . When we had gone through the first sphere that encircles the earth we saw a great light. Then I said to Perpetua who was at my side, 'This is what the Lord has promised us.' We had reached a vast open plain that seemed to be a garden with oleanders and every type of flower. The trees were as tall as cypresses and their leaves sang without ceasing. We arrive at a palace whose walls seem to be made of light. We go in and hear a choir repeating, 'Holy, holy, holy.' In the hall is seated a man clothed in white. He has a youthful face and his hair shines white as snow. On either side of him stand four elders.

We go forward in amazement and we kiss the Lord who caresses us with his hand. The elders say to us, 'Stand up!' We obey and exchange the kiss of peace. . . . We recognise many of the brethren martyrs like us. For food we all had an ineffable perfume that satisfied us wholly.

For the church fathers, miracles are only one reason for arguing that the gospel is true, and not the most compelling reason at that. An even more convincing piece of evidence is the willingness of Christians to die for their faith. Origen regards martyrdom as of equal importance to miracles (*Contra Celsum* 1.31; 3.27; 8.44), and Tertullian declared, 'The oftener we are mown down by you, the more in number we grow; the blood of the martyrs is the seed of the church' (*Ad Nationes* 1.19).

As Bradley puts it, 'When miracles were used to validate the claims of Christianity, they were displayed in the context of a martyr church.'[13] He concludes with this challenge: 'We must unite in prayer that God's Kingdom would be displayed in our midst by signs and wonders, with active concern for justice for the poor and the dispossessed, and a willingness to suffer ourselves when God, in his mercy, calls us to suffer.[14]

The Spirit of glory

We have seen in this final chapter the diverse ways in which the Holy Spirit leads us into closer fellowship with the work of the cross. Through baptism, discipleship, mortification, surrender, hardships, death and martyrdom, the Holy Spirit leads us deeper into the reality and the riches of Calvary. Out of all of these, martyrdom is unquestionably the most challenging. However, the Apostle Peter makes a statement in his first letter which should give great encouragement to those who are called to walk this kind of Calvary road. He says, 'If you are insulted because of the name of Christ, you are blessed, for the Spirit of glory and of God rests on you' (1 Peter 4:14). Many people seek the glorious presence of the Holy Spirit in their lives today. Conferences are held for this purpose. Hundreds of books are written on the subject. But I doubt whether many say what Peter does – that the path to power is persecution. It is in suffering that we find the glory. The way to the Spirit is the cross.

CONCLUSION

Then I heard every creature in heaven and on earth and
under the earth and on the sea, and all that is in them,
singing:

'To him who sits on the throne and to the Lamb
be praise and honour and glory and power,
for ever and ever!'

The four living creatures said, 'Amen,' and the elders fell
down and worshipped.

Revelation 5:13–14

The Triune God is more to be adored than expressed.

T. F. Torrance, *The Ground and Grammar of Theology*[1]

During the second world war, a young second lieutenant
in the Royal Sussex Regiment joined Wingate's British
force known as the 'Chindits'. This force was given the

responsibility to fight behind enemy lines in India, deep in the heart of the jungle. During some fighting at the village of Hintha, this officer was severely wounded. He was so badly injured, in fact, that the column had to proceed without him, and he was left in the jungle, near to death. A Gurkha rifleman known as 'Moto' volunteered to stay behind with him. Every day, Moto would clean his wounds, go to the local villages for food and water, and stand guard at the side of his officer. As the days went by, the wounded officer slowly started to recover.

One day, Moto went off as he usually did, but failed to return. So the officer struggled to his feet and hobbled towards the village of Hintha. He was still very weak, and had to keep stopping for rest. But eventually, after pausing for a drink at a filthy pool of water, he approached the first few houses of the village. He rounded a corner and saw three or four men sitting under the shadow of a tree. For a few seconds the officer stared at them, and they stared at him. Then they sprang to their feet, and as they ran into the light, he saw that they were enemy soldiers. They tied his hands and tried to make him kneel in submission before them. He refused. All he could think about was Moto, so he shouted out at the top of his voice, 'Moto, Moto, they have caught me!' But Moto could not hear. He had already been captured by the Japanese, who knew that he was looking after a British officer somewhere in the jungle. They had asked him where he was, but Moto would not speak. In the end, after torturing Moto, they shot him.

You may wonder why I tell that story. I tell it for two reasons. First of all, I know this story is true because that young British officer was my father, and as a child I used to marvel at the last traces of the wound in his shoulder, where the bullet had entered – a mere centimetre above his heart. Secondly, I tell this story because of the response which my father made to the sacrifice made by this precious Gurkha rifleman. Just after the war, my father wrote this in a book called *Return Via Rangoon*:

> I cannot put into words what I feel about this man. His utter unselfishness in volunteering to stay behind with me, his devotion in looking after me so well and finally, his matchless courage in facing torment and death rather than betray me to the enemy – these are things I cannot trust myself to speak of even today. I can never be worthy of the sacrifice he made but, as long as I live, I shall always have the feeling that my life is not my own, and the memory of Moto will inspire me to the end of my days.[2]

The place of thanksgiving

Every year, I give thanks for Moto on Remembrance Sunday. My wife and four children join me in remembering the sacrifice which Moto made on my father's behalf, and expressing heart-felt gratitude to God for the extraordinary devotion which this man showed.

Every year, Moto's courage reminds me of the one who made an even greater sacrifice, Jesus of Nazareth. It is a love for which we should always be profoundly grateful. It is a sacrifice which should never cease to move us deeply. Indeed, what better words could we use of the cross than those used by my father of Moto's death: 'I can never be worthy of the sacrifice that he made but, as long as I live, I shall always have the feeling that my life is not my own, and his memory will inspire me to the end of my days.'

The sacrificial love of Jesus has been the overarching theme of this book. The crucified Messiah was God's provision; everlasting gratitude should be man's response. With that in mind, I cannot end without a few, all too brief, remarks about the Lord's Supper. In my tradition, we are supposed to have a Holy Communion service every Sunday. For me, every Sunday is therefore a kind of Remembrance Day. As we gather together around the Lord's Table we remember that Jesus is the lamb of God who takes away the sin of the world. As we break bread, we remember the body of Jesus, twisted, bruised and broken for us on the cross. As we pour and drink wine, we remember the blood he shed.

The Lord's Supper is also known as 'the Eucharist'. 'Eucharist' comes from the Greek word *eucharistia*, which means 'thanksgiving'. At the Lord's Table we invite the Holy Spirit to apply once again the finished work of the cross. We should never fail to invite and welcome the presence of the Holy Spirit as we celebrate the Lord's Supper. This invitation, known since ancient times as the *epiclesis* or invocation, is essential. Some people pray a simple prayer, such as, 'Holy Spirit, we welcome you, and we invite you to make this bread and this wine everything Jesus intended it to be'. Others pray more formally, employing a liturgical prayer.

Every celebration of the Lord's Supper is a meal of remembrance. Only the difference is this: we do not merely recall a historical fact. In the Lord's Supper, the Holy Spirit is the invisible guest, bringing revelation of the Calvary love of God, and actualising in our hearts the blessings of the work of the cross. So, as the saying goes, 'while the world drinks to forget, we drink to remember'. As we do so, thanksgiving is released from our lips and our mouths declare and sing praises to God. In other words, our response is not merely intellectual or emotional. It is an expression of our spirits, souls and bodies in response to the Spirit's reminding us of the work of the cross.

Just as a meal should always be preceded by a prayer of

thanksgiving, so gratitude should flow unhindered from our lives as we sit at table with the crucified and risen Jesus. 'Thank you' is the best thing we can say as we receive the benefits of Christ's amazing love. At Calvary, Jesus has demonstrated how much we are worth to him. At the Lord's Table, we should declare how much he is worth to us. As Paul said, 'Thanks be to God for his indescribable gift!' (2 Corinthians 9:15).

The harp and the incense

It is right to give him thanks and praise as we draw to a close now. We have been on a phenomenal journey in this book, exploring the rich relationship between the work of the Spirit and the work of the cross. In these final moments we are discovering one final dimension to this relationship, and this has to do with worship. The Spirit always glorifies the crucified and risen Son. In our worship, he lifts us up into the heavenly realms and reveals the Son of God enthroned on high.

On the Lord's day, John the Apostle was worshipping God in a prison cell on the Roman penal colony of Patmos. Caught up in the power of the Spirit he was invited to enter through a door that was standing open in heaven. As he did so, the Spirit showed him many things. He saw the Father seated on the throne of heaven, holding a scroll in his right hand. A mighty angel asked, 'Who is worthy to open the scroll?' As the citizens of heaven looked around in vain for one who had the right to unroll the parchment and read, John wept and wept as he saw that no one had been found who was worthy. Then Jesus appeared:

I saw a Lamb, looking as if it had been slain, standing in the centre of the throne, encircled by the four living creatures and the elders. He had seven horns and seven eyes, which are the seven spirits of God sent out into all the earth. He came and took the scroll from the right hand of him who sat on the throne. And when he had taken it, the four living creatures and the twenty-four elders fell down before the Lamb. Each one had a harp and they were holding golden bowls full of incense, which are the prayers of the saints. And they sang a new song:

'You are worthy to take the scroll
and to open its seals,
because you were slain,
and with your blood you purchased men for God
from every tribe and language and people and nation.
You have made them to be a kingdom and priests to serve
    our God,
and they will reign on the earth.'

Revelation 5:6–10

And then the angels surrounding the throne began to sing, 'Worthy is the Lamb, who was slain!' (Revelation 5:12).

John, caught up in the Spirit, sees the crucified and risen lamb. Jesus was dead, but he is now alive for evermore. He is risen, ascended, glorified. But even in his exalted state, Jesus is still the lamb of God who looks as if he has been slain. Even though he is risen, Jesus is still the crucified Messiah. Even though he is on the throne of heaven, he still wears the scars of the earth. Jesus is crowned with glory and honour but he still betrays in his body the scars that speak of sacrifice. As the hymn writer once put it:

Crown him the Lord of love;
Behold his hands and side,
Those wounds yet visible above
In beauty glorified;
No angel in the sky

Can fully bear that sight,
But downward bends his burning eye
At mysteries so bright.[3]

It is time to get the harps out and sing love songs to the lamb of God. It is time to release the incense of intercession for the kingdom to come in this world.

This book is now finished. Let the worship begin!

EPILOGUE

What have we discovered about the relationship between the work of the Spirit and the work of the cross? If I were to summarise the findings, they would read thus:

- The Holy Spirit was at work in the lives of the Old Testament prophets and priests, revealing the future sufferings of Christ on the cross.
- The Holy Spirit enabled and empowered Jesus to offer up his life as a perfect sacrifice at Calvary.
- The Holy Spirit is poured out in a wholly new way as a direct result of Jesus' willingness to be lifted up on the cross.
- The Holy Spirit now applies the benefits of the cross in salvation – the new covenant established through the blood of Christ and the Spirit's fire.
- The Holy Spirit confirms and accompanies the preaching of the cross in demonstrations of supernatural power, including healing and deliverance.
- The Holy Spirit takes us into fellowship with the cross through baptism, discipleship, mortification, surrender, hardship, death and martyrdom.

In the prologue to this book I described the introduction to

Jesus in John's Gospel. John the Baptist declares him to be the lamb of God and the one who baptises in the Holy Spirit. In the space of a few moments, John encapsulates everything I have tried to say in this book about the work of the cross and the work of the Spirit. What God has joined together, let no one divide!

Not long ago, Jan Mungeam wrote the following. It struck me as a timely testimony, and I end with it here. Like John the Baptist's words, it embraces the main theme and findings of this book:

The Lord often speaks to me through dreams. When for some weeks he had been silent in this respect, I asked him to reveal something from his heart. A few nights later I had a most simple and yet most profound dream. In the sky I saw what seemed like hundreds of thousands of shimmering bright (but miniature) angels move from a shapeless 'flock' into the shape of the cross. After a while the cross disappeared whilst the shiny beings formed into the shape of a dove. After some moments it too disappeared and I woke with a tremendous sense of the presence of the Lord and the value of both these interventions of God in history. *The finished work of Jesus on the cross and the ongoing work of the Holy Spirit are at the heart of our lives and ministry.*

NOTES

Introduction

1. Tom Smail, *Once and For All. A Confession of the Cross* (London: Darton, Longman & Todd, 1998), p.6.
2. Andrew Murray, *The Cross of Christ* (London: Marshall Morgan & Scott [first published in book form 1989]), p.26.
3. For more on this, see Tom Smail, *op. cit.*, p.16.
4. Mark Stibbe, *Times of Refreshing* (London: Marshall Pickering, 1995).
5. Andrew Murray, *op. cit.*, p. 26.

Chapter 1

1. George Eldon Ladd, *A Theology of the New Testament* (Grand Rapids, Michigan: Eerdmans, 1974), p.57.
2. Quoted in Josh McDowell, *Christianity. A Ready Defence* (San Bernadino, California: Here's Life Publishers, 1990), pp.212–213.
3. Alfred Edersheim, *The Life and Times of Jesus the Messiah* (Peabody, Massachusetts: Hendrickson Publishers, 1993), p.896.
4. Samuel Levine, *You Take Jesus, I'll Take God* (Hamoroh

Press, 1980), pp.24–25.

5. See Carsten Peter Thiede, *The Dead Sea Scrolls and the Jewish Origins of Christianity* (Oxford: Lion Publishing, 2000), pp.195–197.

6. I am indebted to Mark Eastman and Chuck Smith for these insights. See their co-authored book, *The Search for the Messiah* (Costa Mesa, California: The Word for Today, 1993), pp.11–27 (chapter 2, on 'The Suffering Servant'). Their findings are in turn based on research by Alfred Edersheim, *op. cit.*, pp.980–1010.

7. Rabbi Professor Dan Cohn-Sherbok, 'The Master of the Universe', the *Church Times*, 7 June 1996, p.11.

8. Professor David Berger, quoted in Cohn-Sherbok, above, p.11.

9. This quotation is from an article entitled, 'The Dead Sea Scrolls', written by Professor Vermes, printed in the *Church Times*, 1995.

Chapter 2

1. Madeleine Caron Rock, 'He is the Lonely Greatness of the World', cited in *The Poet's Christ*, compiled by David Winter (Oxford: Lion Publishers, 1998), p.95.

2. See chapter 5 of Martin Hengel's *Crucifixion* (London: SCM Press, 1977), pp.33–38. Cicero called crucifixion *summum supplicium*, the supreme penalty (*In Verrem* 2.5.168).

3. Melito, *Homily on the Passion*, 96f, quoted in Martin Hengel, *op. cit.*, p.21.

4. I am indebted in what follows to William D. Edwards, Wesley J. Gabel and Floyd E. Hosmer, and their excellent article 'On the Physical Death of Jesus Christ' in the *Journal for the American Medical Association*, March 1986, Volume 255, issue 11, pp.1455–1463.

5. Gerald Hawthorne, *The Presence and the Power. The Significance of the Holy Spirit in the Ministry of Jesus* (Dallas, Texas: Word Publishing, 1991), p.113.
6. Tom Smail, *Once and For All*, p.70.
7. Quotation taken from a sermon by Minka Shura Sprague, published on the Internet.
8. Gordon Fee, *God's Empowering Presence. The Holy Spirit in the Letters of Paul* (Peabody, Massachusetts: Hendrickson Publishers, 1994), p.644.

Chapter 3

1. Andrew Murray, *The Cross of Christ*, p.14.
2. See in particular Barbara Richmond, *Jewish Insights into the New Testament* (Titusville, Florida: Thunderbird Press, 1996), pp.43–46.
3. Many interpreters would not agree with the NIV translation. The word 'Spirit', they would argue, should not have a capital letter. It does not refer to the Spirit but to the resurrected state of Christ. In other words, Jesus was put to death in the natural realm of the flesh and made alive in the supernatural, spirit realm. Either interpretation is, however, permissible, though the second may be more logical on grammatical grounds.
4. See for example Romans 1:4. It is interesting to ask what the Holy Spirit was doing between the time of Jesus' death and the moment of the resurrection. Blaine Charette has a perspective on this. In his study of the Holy Spirit in Matthew's Gospel (*Restoring Presence*. Sheffield: Sheffield Academic Press, 2000), Charette proposes that the Holy Spirit leaves Jesus' body at the moment of death ('he let go the S/spirit' [Matthew 27:50]) and then, in fulfilment of Ezekiel 37:1–14, raised the holy ones in Jerusalem (pp.92–96). 'Some remark-

able, effective power breaks forth at the moment of Jesus' death' (p.94 – the rending of the temple veil and the resurrection of the saints).

5. Tom Smail, 'The Cross and the Spirit', in *Charismatic Renewal: The Search for a Theology* (London: SPCK, 1993), pp.54–55.

6. Words attributed to William Rees.

7. Andrew Murray, *The Cross of Christ*, p.18.

Chapter 4

1. Jonathan Edwards, *Jonathan Edwards on Revival* (Edinburgh: The Banner of Truth Trust, 1995), p.110.

2. Max Allan Collins, *Saving Private Ryan* (a novel based on Robert Rodat's Screenplay) (London: Penguin Books, 1998), p.311.

3. *Ibid.*, p.317.

4. For more on this, see Tom Smail, *Once and for All*, chapter 3. I like very much the way Tom puts it on p.52: 'If our Reformation forebears saw themselves as sinners rather than victims and if we in our day see ourselves as victims rather than sinners, the truth may be that we are always both.'

5. Jurgen Moltmann, trans. R. A. Wilson and J. Bowden, *The Crucified God* (London: SCM Press Ltd, 1974).

6. A line from the hymn 'And Can it Be', written by Charles Wesley (1707-1788).

7. Tom Smail, *Once and For All*, p.49.

8. Gordon Fee, *Paul, the Spirit, and the People of God* (London: Hodder & Stoughton, 1997), p.44.

9. It should be noted that there are different versions of the 'order of salvation'. Some would argue that we should not tie the Spirit down in this way. In other words, surely the experience of entering our salvation

is more supra-rational than this? However, there are certain constants within the various facets of our Christian beginnings. The version offered here is one that I personally believe makes good sense of Scripture and experience.

10. Published in the summer issue 2000 of *Joy Magazine*.

11. Wayne Grudem, *Systematic Theology* (Grand Rapids, Michigan: Zondervan, 1994), p.692. Grudem's *ordo salutis* differs from mine. He has election, effectual calling, regeneration, conversion, justification, adoption, sanctification, perseverance, death and glorification. I have problems with the word 'conversion' because I don't find it in Scripture (though I accept that it can be used in a discussion like this). Also, my version is much shorter because in this context I am merely interested in our entrance into salvation. Grudem is obviously interested in the present and future tenses of salvation as well.

12. For more on this, see my book *Thinking Clearly About Revival* (London: Monarch Books, 1998), pp.24–26.

13. Rodman Williams, *Renewal Theology*, Volume 2 (Grand Rapids, Michigan: Zondervan, 1990), p.64. Anyone interested in developing a coherent charismatic/pentecostal theology cannot afford to do without Williams' three volumes. Notice the simplicity of his *ordo salutis*. For Williams, entering salvation consists of only three stages: calling, regeneration and justification. This may be too simple, however, and it downplays the critical importance of adoption as a distinct and vital link in the chain of grace.

14. Wayne Grudem, *Systematic Theology* p.726. I love the way Grudem describes and portrays the two ideas of imputation (the non-imputation of sin, and the imputation of Christ's righteousness). He portrays the

non-imputation of sin as follows:

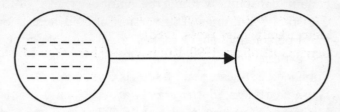

Here the first circle is our state before salvation. Our spiritual account is full of minus signs. However, as we are justified, God declares our account cleared. He does not reckon or impute our sins to us.

But this is not the end. Not only do we have the joy of the non-imputation of sin, we have the glory of the imputation of Christ's righteousness. So we go from a blank circle to a circle of plus signs:

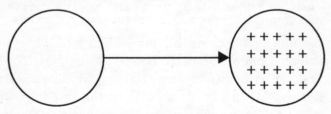

This is a great way of explaining simply the wonderful truth of justification by faith (p.725).

15. Quoted in John Armstrong's book, *Five Great Evangelists. Preachers of Real Revival* (Fearn, Ross-shire: Christian Focus Publications, 1997), p.93.

16. *From Orphans to Heirs. Celebrating our Spiritual Adoption* (Oxford: Bible Reading Fellowship, 1999).

17. Quoted in Ed Plorek's book, *The Father Loves You. An Invitation to Perfect Love* (Cape Town, South Africa: Vineyard International Publishing, 1999), p.99. Sadly, Plorek doesn't give the reference in Luther's writings.

18. For an academic study on this subject, see Charles Cosgrove's *The Cross and the Spirit: A Study in the Argument and Theology of Galatians* (Macon, Georgia: Mercer University Press, 1988).

19. Gerrit Gufstafson, 1990, Kingsway's Thank You Music.

Chapter 5

1. Tom Marshall, *Free Indeed. Fullness for the Whole Man – Spirit, Soul and Body* (Tonbridge, Kent: Sovereign World Ltd, 1975), p.121. Tom Marshall was originally asked to write a book on 'the work of the cross and the work of the Spirit'. However, he died in 1993 before he had really begun the project.

2. Jonathan Edwards, *Jonathan Edwards on Revival*, p.44.

3. *Ibid*, p.109.

4. Robert Gundry writes: 'Some think that Isaiah spoke only figuratively in 53:4; ie, sicknesses and pains that stand for sins. Along with forgiveness of sins, however, physical well-being was thought to characterise the messianic age (cf. Isaiah 29:18; 32:3–4; 35:5–6).' Gundry speaks here of 'Matthew's literalism'. Matthew does not spiritualise 'infirmities and diseases' (Robert H Gundry, *Matthew*. [Grand Rapids, Michigan: Eerdmans, 1982], p.150). They plainly refer to physical illnesses.

5. Matthew knew the Greek version of the Old Testament known as the Septuagint (LXX) but did not always choose to use it in his gospel. Sometimes he provided his own Greek translation of the Hebrew version of the Old Testament. Matthew 8:17 is a case in point. Here the gospel writer departs from the LXX in his translation of the Hebrew version of Isaiah 53:4. Unlike the LXX, Matthew uses verbs that imply removal rather than carrying. Most commentaries point this out (see

W D Davies and Dale C Allison, *A Critical and Exegetical Commentary on the Gospel According to St Matthew. Vol.2.* [Edinburgh: T & T Clark, 1991], pp.37–38). The two verbs that Matthew uses here, *lambano* and *bastazo*, do not denote 'carrying' but 'removal', as all the recent studies of this passage show. Matthew will therefore not allow us to believe that Jesus carried our sicknesses in the same way that he bore our sins. Jesus did not become sick in the same way that he became sin. Though healing is in the atonement, it is not guaranteed in the same way that the forgiveness of sins is. Healing is one of the benefits of the cross, often applied now, but only completely realised in the new heaven and the new earth.

6. Leon Morris, *The Cross of Jesus* (Carlisle, UK: The Paternoster Press, 1988), p.93.

7. See footnote 6 of chapter 4.

8. The only book in English on Hauge currently in print is Joseph Shaw's excellent study, *Pulpit Under the Sky. A Life of Hans Nielsen Hauge* (Wesport, CT: Greenwood Press, 1979). There are a number of studies in Norwegian currently in print, which my wife Alie has read as part of a dissertation that she is doing on Hauge. I am indebted to her here. For Hauge's conversion, see Shaw, pp.21–23.

9. Joseph Shaw, *Pulpit Under the Sky*, p.26.

Chapter 6

1. Rich Nathan and Ken Wilson, *Empowered Evangelicals. Bringing Together the Best of the Evangelical and Charismatic Worlds* (Ann Arbor, Michigan: Vine Books, 1995), p.65 and p.70

2. Joseph Shaw, *Pulpit Under the Sky*, pp.140–142.

3. I am very grateful to my dear friend Marc Dupont for sharing this dream of his with me.

4. For a more detailed exploration of this phenomenon and its implications, see Robert Mansfield, *Spirit and Gospel in Mark* (Peabody, MA: Hendrickson, 1987), and George Montague, 'The Spirit and the Cross: Mark', *The Holy Spirit: Growth of a Biblical Tradition* (Peabody, MA: Hendrickson, 1993).

5. Dietrich Bonhoeffer, *The Cost of Discipleship* (first published in German in 1937, and translated by R.H.Fuller) (London: SCM Press, 1980), p.35f. 'Cheap grace' is receiving the gift of God's love and then living a life of cost-free commitment. It is exactly what I am trying to combat in this chapter: the tendency of many Protestants to rest on the pardon of their justification without then pursuing radical holiness. It is the tendency to enjoy the benefits of the *fact* of the cross without engaging in all the daily challenges of our *fellowship* in the cross.

6. Quoted in Andrew Murray, *The Cross of Christ*, p.64.

7. Michael Duggan, 'The Cross and the Spirit in Paul: Implications for Baptism in the Holy Spirit', in *Pneuma: The Journal for the Society for Pentecostal Studies 7.2*, Fall 1985, p.144.

8. See Mark Stibbe, *Revival* (The *Thinking Clearly* series), pp.172–173.

9. J. W. Van Deventer and W. S. Weeden.

10. Andrew Murray, *The Cross of Christ*, p.3.

11. Jonathan Edwards, *Jonathan Edwards on Revival*, pp.55–63.

12. James Bradley, 'Miracles and Martyrdom in the Early Church', in H. Hunter and P. Hocken, eds, *Altogether in One Place* (Sheffield: Sheffield Academic Press, 1993), pp.227–241.

13. *Ibid* p.241.
14. *Ibid* p.241.

Conclusion

1. T. F. Torrance, *The Ground and Grammar of Theology* (Belfast: Christian Journals Ltd, 1980), p.167.
2. Philip Stibbe, *Return Via Rangoon* (London: Newman Wolsey Ltd, 1947), p.130. This book has recently been republished by Leo Cooper.
3. Matthew Bridges and Godfrey Thring.